EVERYTHING YOU NEED TO KNOW

SHARK WEEK

BY MARTHA BROCKENBROUGH

The author would like to thank Adam Berliant for his assistance with data analysis, Lish McBride for her work in pitting sharks against other predators, and Michael Heithaus and Linda Richmond Heithaus for their generosity, insight, and information about sharks.

A FEIWEL AND FRIENDS BOOK

An Imprint of Macmillan

Printed in the United States of America by R. R. Donnelley & Sons Company, Willard, Ohio.
For information, address Feiwel and Friends, 175 Fifth Avenue, New York, N.Y. 10010.

Our books may be purchased in bulk for promotional, educational, or business use. Please contact your local bookseller or the Macmillan Corporate and Premium Sales Department at (800) 221-7945 ext. 5442 or by e-mail at MacmillanSpecialMarkets@macmillan.com.

Library of Congress Cataloging-in-Publication Data Available

ISBN: 978-1-250-09777-4 (hardcover)
2 4 6 8 10 9 7 5 3 1

ISBN: 978-1-250-09778-1 (paperback)
2 4 6 8 10 9 7 5 3 1

Book design by April Ward

Feiwel and Friends logo designed by Filomena Tuosto

First Edition: 2016

mackids.com

CONTENTS

You might already love sharks. Maybe you're one of the 45 million people who watched Shark Week programming on Discovery. If you had your way, you'd make every week shark week. We know just how you feel.

But it's also possible that sharks scare you—at least a bit. And that's okay, too. As predators go, few are more powerful or better adapted to take down prey.

The truth is, sharks might be the most misunderstood animals on the planet. Maybe it's because we've watched *Jaws* or other scary shark movies. Maybe it's because we've read news stories about attacks on swimmers and surfers. Or maybe because we've so often heard them described as glassy-eyed, mindless eating machines that like nothing more

than the taste of human flesh. Whatever the reason, we fear these animals more than we should.

There's a word for this excessive fear of sharks: *galeophobia*. It's made of two Greek words: *phobos*, which means "fear," and *galeos*, which is a kind of shark with weasel-like markings. A kind of funny thing about this word: *galeophobia* is also used for fear of polecats, weasels, and skunks—all animals with the contrasting dark-and-light coloring found on many sharks.

Whatever the reason for your galeophobia, you can in all likelihood let it go. You're a whole lot more likely to win the lottery than you are to be bitten by a shark—and you're almost certainly not going to win the lottery. (Sorry.)

If you want to fear an animal, fear the mosquito. The World Health Organization says this tiny bloodsucker kills more than 1 million people a year by transmitting malaria through its bites. No other animal kills as many humans—or comes even close—except other people.

Lightning strikes are vastly deadlier than sharks, and we know how rare those are. Best estimates put their death toll at as many as 24,000 people per year.

Meanwhile, what's cuter than a white-tailed deer? Not much. And yet these adorable forest dwellers kill around 130 people a year—way more than sharks do. Granted, it's when people's cars hit the deer, which is usually at least as hard on the deer as it is on the humans. But still, as these things go, Bambi is far more of a statistical menace. If you want to spend any of your worry points on death by animal, you should fear the deer

Here are the facts: hardly anyone dies in shark attacks, and most people who sustain bites survive. In the past decade an average of about six people around the world have been killed each year by sharks, according to the International Shark Attack File, which began in 1958 and has tracked more than 3,400 incidents since the mid-1500s to the present day. Of people bitten by sharks each year, most—around 65—survive.

Shark attacks are bad, of course. But they are rare enough that you shouldn't spend any time at all worrying about them. If you know sharks are in the water, don't go swimming. If you see them, don't provoke or feed them. You'd be surprised how many people do that. We'll get to that in Chapter 5.

The bottom line is, sharks are a creature to cheer, not fear. They're remarkable in so many ways. Here are just a few:

- They have flexible cartilage instead of bones.

- There are more than 500 species of shark.

- Their teeth continuously replace themselves.

- Their giant livers help them float.

- They can sense electric fields given off by animals, objects, and water moving through the earth's magnetic field.

- They evolved 200 million years *before* dinosaurs. They're older than insects, amphibians, reptiles—even older than seeds and flowers. (Human beings are a lot younger, only about 200,000 years old as a species.)

Whatever you want to know about sharks, chances are you can find out in this book, which is named for the wildly popular Discovery show.

We cover everything from how, when, and where they attack to the specialization of their anatomy that makes them such fierce and wonderful hunters.

We talk about how and where they are born, live, and die. And even who their biggest enemies are. You might just be surprised to find out what kills as many as 200 million sharks every year—and why.

We dive deep into the anatomies and oddities of some of the most fantastic of all sharks—even extinct ones.

We pit them in imaginary battles against some of your other favorite predators. Sharks are fearsome, yes. They are some of the world's most efficient and skilled hunters. But there are also many reasons to love them—and turn your galeophobia to galeomania.

SHARK WEEK

CHAPTER ONE

SHARK LIFE—
THE INS AND OUTS OF A SHARK'S WORLD

HOW LONG SHARKS HAVE LIVED

By any measure, sharks are magnificent animals. They're older than dinosaurs. They can grow larger than elephants. They're powerful hunters—the biggest, strongest, and fastest fish in the sea. The more you know about these creatures, the more you will admire them.

A few facts to start with:

THEY'RE AN ANCIENT CREATURE. The earliest-known shark fossils are more than 400 million years old. The oldest-known dinosaur fossil is 240 million years old. The shark is a survivor, evolved to inhabit every ocean of the world. Sharks have out-lasted dinosaurs and giant mammals and, with care from humanity, might continue to thrive.

THEY'RE DIVERSE. The tiniest are a few inches long. The biggest can grow up to 45 feet.

THEY CAN LIVE LONG LIVES. Some can live a century—sharks alive today might have been around, for example, when the *Titanic* sank.

SIGHT

HEARING

TASTE

HUMAN SENSES

TOUCH

SMELL

THEY HAVE SENSES THAT HUMANS DON'T. Think about how much information you glean from your senses. Touch. Taste. Hearing. Smell. Sight. Sharks can do all of that (and in many cases better than we can). Plus, they can sense vibrations in the water and the electricity generated by living things.

SHARK EVOLUTION

Sharks have had the same basic body shape and structure for hundreds of millions of years: a head, a body, a tail, gills, and fins. This doesn't mean sharks haven't changed over time; they have, and some species have evolved in spectacular ways. And the idea that sharks are "living fossils" is being modified the more we know about them. Some sharks are similar to extinct ones. But many modern sharks have more advanced gills than extinct sharks, according to a team of researchers led by the American Museum of Natural History.

We're only learning this now because there aren't a lot of fossilized gill arches, and because older technology didn't let us study these as closely

as newer devices. In short, sharks are complicated, highly evolved, and worthy of close study to understand not only them, but also how things like jaws and human hearing evolved.

Some people mistakenly believe evolution is an unproven theory. This is not the case. Evolution describes the way living things change over time and pass changes on to their offspring. There are theories about *how* this happens, and one of the most fundamental is natural selection: traits that help species survive long enough to reproduce are the ones that are passed on.

Whatever the mechanism for evolution, the key central idea is that all life on earth shares a common ancestor. We are all connected, even if we are not all the same.

Each vertebrate—a classification that includes mammals, birds, fish, reptiles, amphibians, and fish—is descended from tiny, simple creatures that developed in the oceans during the Cambrian period, about 500 million years ago.

Over tens of millions of years, these animals became more fishlike, developing a backbone, fins, and mouths that could be used to scoop food.

Around 400 million years ago, these fish ancestors split into two groups: bony fish and cartilaginous fish.

Sharks, which don't have bones, come from the cartilaginous line. There are some sharks alive today that are amazingly similar to sharks that lived 150 million years ago. Rays and chimaeras are also cartilaginous fish, and there are about 1,100 species of those we know of. You can think of those as close relatives to the shark. Cartilaginous fish are less common than bony fish, which come in about 25,000 varieties. That said, we discover new animals all the time, and it's certain that very rare species become extinct without ever being discovered—so these numbers are best guesses.

BASIC FACTS

HOW MANY KINDS OF SHARKS ARE THERE?

Possibly more than 500 species.

HOW LONG DO SHARKS LIVE?

Different species have different life spans. Also, sharks in captivity don't live as long as sharks in the wild (possibly because they don't get to swim around as much).

The more we learn about shark behavior, including migration patterns, the more we will know about their life spans. Scientists today are using GPS to track sharks and learn this—and more—information.

Here are a few life-span ranges:

GREAT WHITE SHARK: These creatures live 70 years or more, a lot like humans. This is much longer than we previously thought, according to a 2014 study conducted at Woods Hole Oceanographic Institution in Massachusetts.

It's tricky to determine how old a shark is (you can't exactly ask).

One method is to look at a shark's skeleton and count the "rings" of cartilage. This isn't a perfect system, though. As with tree rings, the shark rings vary in width and can be difficult to distinguish.

The Woods Hole study used this technique and the remnants of nuclear bomb testing conducted in the 1950s and 1960s to measure the life span of great whites. These nuclear weapons tests produced something called carbon-14, a radioactive variant of carbon. Marine animals alive during those tests absorbed the unusual isotope, so it stands out like a flag where it's present. The biggest male shark they examined was 73 years old, based on the rings they counted before and after those nuclear test years. The oldest female was 40, which could mean female sharks don't live as long, but not necessarily. Discovery has footage of what is believed to be a pregnant 50-year-old great white, so it seems just as likely they simply didn't find an older female.

WHALE SHARK: The biggest surviving species of shark might also have a supersize life span. One way to guess a shark's life span is to study when it is able to reproduce. This happens at the 20 percent marker of their life span. Male whale sharks can breed when they're about 30 years old. This would be 20 percent of a 150-year life span.

TIGER SHARK: They can live up to 50 years in the wild. Their reproduction rates are slow, which is typical of animals with long life spans. It's worrisome with the tiger shark, though, which is a target for its fins, skin, flesh, and liver. Because they are such a popular catch, they are listed as a near-threatened species everywhere they live.

HOW FAST ARE SHARKS?

Sharks are phenomenal swimmers. There are three components of swimming: lift; balance and steering; and forward motion, which comes from pushing water backward.

Sharks get lift from their very oily and fatty livers (unlike fish, which have a little balloon of air inside of them).

They get their balance and steering from their fins.

Their forward motion comes from their powerful tails, which swing from side to side.

A shark's shape is related to its speed. The fastest sharks are the most aerodynamic in shape—like torpedoes. They have tail fins that are more symmetrical. Slower sharks are longer and thinner, and their tail lobes tend to be asymmetrical.

Researchers studied the side-to-side motion of the tail fins of spiny dogfish and chain dogfish. By putting small particles in water and using lasers to reflect light off the particles, the scientists discovered that shark tails generate twice as many jets of water as other fish tails. In other words, their tails are pushing more water backward—it's like having a more powerful engine.

So how do these dogfish do it? They stiffen their tails mid-swing. The behavior gives sharks almost continuous forward thrust.

SHORTFIN MAKO SHARK: This is the fastest shark. Speed estimates vary, though some estimates clock it at 60 miles per hour over short distances. Unlike many sharks, which have a bigger top lobe on their tail fin, the mako's is nearly symmetrical. The short-fin mako has to be fast. It eats tuna, swordfish, other sharks, and squid—all speedy movers.

Asymmetrical caudal fin

GREENLAND SHARK: This is the slowest-known shark—at least for its size. It's also the slowest-known fish, inch for inch. They swim at 1.7 miles per hour, the pace of a leisurely walk. They achieve this speed by swinging their tails a mere nine times per minute, according to a study from the National Institute of Polar Research.

One reason these big sharks are so poky is they live in very cold water. Their pokiness doesn't prevent them from eating the much-faster seals, though. Seals sleep underwater, probably to stay safe from polar bears. This makes them an easy catch.

MOST SURPRISING TRAVELING HABITS: For the longest time, we thought tiger sharks were a coastal species. But a recent study from Nova Southeastern University's Guy Harvey Research Institute in Florida shows otherwise.

These animals are long-distance travelers, moving every year between the coral reefs of the Caribbean to the open waters of the mid–North Atlantic Ocean. What's more, they spend winters in the same spot each year, which makes habitat preservation crucial.

Some shark migration patterns are even more complex. Shark species that reproduce every two years have been tagged and found to follow two-year migration patterns. These return to pupping grounds every other year to have babies.

The biggest-known shark migration in US waters happens on Florida's Atlantic coast. Five-foot-long blacktip sharks cruise by the coast in the winter, sometimes in groups of thousands. They're heading for bays and estuaries where they will mate and have pups. These are the source of some unprovoked shark bites in Florida (none were fatal, and experts believe they happened when sharks confused swimmers with food).

WHERE DO SHARKS LIVE?

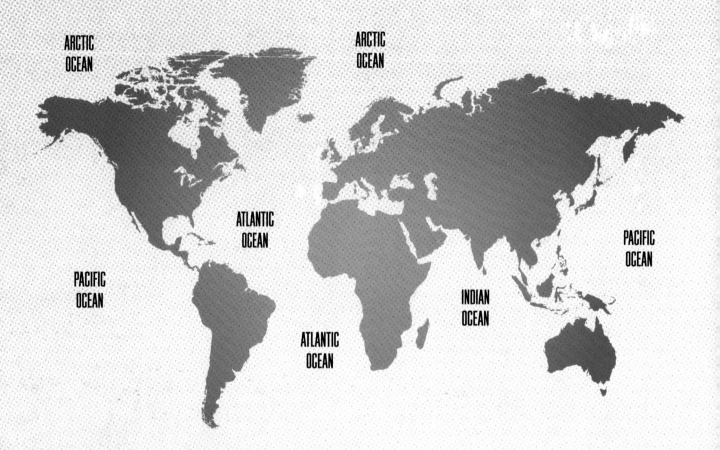

There are two ways of looking at a shark's habitat: which bodies of water they inhabit, and where in the water they reside—near the surface, in the depths of the ocean, or at the bottom of shallower waters.

Sharks are in every ocean around the world (though not in all parts of all oceans). They aren't in Antarctica, but warmer waters brought about by climate change might make it possible for them to survive there. Some sharks can even survive in freshwater rivers.

One of the most famous sharks, the great white, is also found in the most places. They can live in shallow coastal waters and the deep ocean, and in tropical and even subpolar waters.

COLD, SHALLOW COASTAL WATERS: This is the preferred environment for sevengill sharks. These sharks are slow moving and prefer continental shelves, bays, and fjords that are 160 feet deep or less. They keep to the bottom.

WARM COASTAL REGIONS, TROPICAL AND TEMPERATE SEAS: Tiger sharks love these environments and swim thousands of miles from continent to continent. You won't find them in the Mediterranean, though.

Hammerheads also like warm and tropical waters around the globe. They're sometimes near the shore and sometimes in the open sea, and they can skim the surface or dive 1,000 feet deep. Some have even been found living near an underwater volcano.

THE OPEN SEA: Oceanic whitetips sometimes travel closer to land, but generally are found in warm waters in the ocean.

WHO LIKES IT COLD? The big, slow-moving Greenland shark can take the frigid waters of the North Atlantic. You'll also find them near Iceland.

HOW BIG CAN THEY GET?

There are hundreds of species of sharks, each of which comes in a range of sizes. Female sharks are often bigger than males.

THE BIGGEST: The biggest sharks can be almost as long as school buses (which are 45 feet).

These are whale sharks, slow-moving, gentle giants that eat plankton and tiny fish by swimming along with their mouths open and vacuuming their meals from the upper layer of the tropical seas they inhabit.

They range in size on average from 18 to 30 feet, though they can get larger. They also weigh around 20 tons, or more than 40,000 pounds.

THE SMALLEST: While there are many sharks you could hold in your palm, a rare creature called a pale catshark might just be the tiniest one. A single, young female catshark that measured a little over eight inches long was found near Indonesia. These are so rare scientists do not yet know how big (or small) the average one is.

Another tiny and spectacular shark is the green lanternshark, which is believed to live in the northwest Atlantic Ocean, in the northern Gulf of Mexico and Caribbean, and maybe also Brazil. These small sharks are just over 10 inches long. Little is known about this species, which has tiny, light-producing organs on its sides.

HOW DO SHARKS SWIM?

Sharks are flexible because they don't have bony skeletons. They get their structure from light and bendy cartilage. They move when their powerful side muscles contract, one side at a time. They're powered by their caudal, or tail, fins.

If you were to watch one from above, you'd see them curve in a bit of an S shape. But too much bending would be inefficient, so they stiffen their bodies and make less of that S shape once they get going.

Surprisingly, some sharks walk, sometimes as much as they swim. These sharks tend to have muscular front fins that they use to walk around the seafloor, and sometimes—in the case of bamboo sharks—they'll even scoot from one tide pool to another, crawling out of the water as they do.

HOW DO THEY BREATHE?

Most sharks have five gills. The ones with six—called sixgills—are believed to be more primitive, because they resemble fossils of the oldest sharks. These tend to be big, about the size of great whites. They're also hard to find because they stay deep in the ocean, away from light.

Some sharks have spiracles, which are special gills that provide oxygen to the eyes and brain. These are right behind the shark's eye.

Unlike bony fish, shark gills don't have gill coverings.

All sharks need water moving over their gills to breathe and stay alive. But not all sharks do this the same way.

Certain ones swim fast with their mouths open. This kind of breathing is called ram ventilation.

Other kinds of sharks, especially the slower swimmers, have muscles in their mouths that suck

in water and wash it over their gills. This means they can stay still and continue to breathe. This is called buccal pumping, named after the buccal muscles in the mouth.

Some sharks can switch breathing types. Others, including the great white, mako, and whale shark, can't and must keep moving to keep oxygen flowing in and carbon dioxide flowing out.

HOW DO THEY STAY AFLOAT?

Bony fish have an airbag inside that keeps them from sinking. Think of it as nature's equivalent to those inflatable floaties some small children use when swimming.

Sharks don't have airbags. They've evolved other ways of achieving buoyancy. Part of this comes from their lightweight, cartilaginous skeletons.

Part of it, though, comes from their livers. These store lightweight oils, and in deepwater sharks, about a quarter of the animal's weight comes from this oil. (They also help sharks store energy.)

Sand tigers have a do-it-yourself air bag. They gulp air at the surface and hold it in their stomachs. This helps them hover in the water without moving.

WHAT DO THEY EAT?

Sharks mostly eat smaller fish, but some sharks eat seals, sea lions, and other marine mammals.

The biggest sharks—whale sharks—eat tiny food, including plankton, which is a name given to a wide variety of small sea life that drift in ocean currents (they can't swim against it). Plankton can be plants, animals, and even bacteria.

No sharks are strict vegetarians. No sharks are evolved to eat people, either, though it has on very rare occasions happened.

ARE SHARKS WARM- OR COLD-BLOODED?

Most fish are cold-blooded. Some sharks, though, are able to keep their body temperature higher than the water they swim in. Their powerful muscles generate heat while they're swimming. For most sharks, this heat dissipates when their blood flows through their gills, which are always bringing in cold water from the sea. Sharks that can hang on to this warmth, like white sharks and porbeagles, have a hunting advantage. The heat-keepers don't do this with blubber, like whales and other aquatic mammals. Instead, they've evolved two sets of blood vessels that work together to hold in heat. Called capillaries, the blood vessels carrying oxygen-rich blood that's been chilled by the sea run in the opposite direction of other blood vessels carrying blood that's been warmed by the shark's activity. It's like holding a cold hand in a warm hand—the heat exchange warms the cold hand right up.

HOW SHARKS ARE BORN

Animal reproduction is a fascinating subject. It's also one that we don't study enough (probably because people think it's embarrassing and gross).

One scientific journal that studies how animals reproduce tracked 12,000 studies over a ten-year period. They discovered that 90 percent of the studies looked at the same species: mice, rats, and cows.

We're missing out. Reproduction is a wonder. For example, sea horse dads are the ones who get pregnant and go through labor (and can have up to 1,500 babies at a time).

Reproduction can also happen in many different ways. Sometimes it requires two parents. This is almost but not always the case with more complex animals.

Sometimes animals that reproduce with two parents can also reproduce on their own. Creatures called brittle stars do this. They can break off parts and grow a new self. This is asexual reproduction (although they can reproduce with a partner).

Some life-forms only reproduce on their own, copying themselves as they do. For example, a kind of microscopic green algae called a volvox lives in pond water. It forms bubbles of thousands of clone cells. These colonies reach a certain size, and then they fall apart, and start over.

Reproduction is not only interesting, it's also really important. We can't prevent endangered species from going extinct if we don't know how, when, and where they have their babies. What's more, knowing how other animals reproduce might help humans who are having trouble bearing children.

HOW SHARKS MATE

Animals have evolved many ways of reproducing themselves. Some, like birds, lay eggs. Some, like mammals, give birth to live offspring. Sharks—incredible survival machines that they are—do both.

The three types of shark reproduction have one thing in common: the eggs are fertilized when they're still inside the female shark.

Other fish fertilize their eggs on the outside, after the female has laid them. This means they have to lay a lot more eggs to have enough survive.

Internal fertilization requires a bit of courtship. This doesn't always go well for the male shark. When the female signals her acceptance, the male deposits the sperm inside the female.

This part of the experience isn't exactly a Hollywood romance, at least in the shark matings researchers have observed. With larger species of

shark, the male bites the female. This is why female sharks have thicker skin than males. It protects them.

After the male bites the female's back or dorsal fin, he uses a specialized extension of his pelvic fin, called a clasper, to deposit packages of sperm into her reproductive tract. This is how you can tell a male shark from a female, by the way. Only the males have claspers.

Female sharks can be fertilized by more than one male shark at a time. After that, gestation can take from five months to two years. That sharks fertilize their eggs internally and often gestate them there too is one of the things that help shark pups survive.

Some sharks we don't know well enough to know for sure how they reproduce. But they fall into these three categories:

OVIPAROUS: Sharks that reproduce this way lay eggs not long after mating. The eggs develop as they are anchored to seabeds in shark nurseries.

The eggs each contain one shark embryo, which is protected in a shell made from keratin, the same protein that makes your hair and fingernails, as well as the hooves, feathers, claws, and horns of some other animals.

The eggs are laid in pairs. As the baby shark grows, it is nourished by the yolk through an umbilical cord. Developing shark pups breathe when they're in these egg cases. The cases have slits, and the baby sharks swing their tails so that water flows through.

Hatching can take up to a year. The sharks emerge as fully formed, miniature versions of their parents.

About 40 percent of sharks lay eggs.

APLACENTAL VIVIPAROUS: With this type of reproduction, the shark egg hatches *inside* the mother.

After mating, a shark mother gestates the egg in her uterus. Each fertilized egg, or embryo, develops into a purselike object. The yolk of the egg feeds the growing pup. When that's gone, the growing sharks sometimes get nutrition from the lining of the uterus. They also sometimes get it from eating their brothers and sisters.

Gestation can take up to two years before the sharks hatch into their mother's body and emerge fully developed.

About 30 percent of sharks reproduce this way.

VIVIPAROUS: The remainder of sharks—about 27 percent—reproduce like mammals do. Embryos develop in a uterus and are fed by a placenta. Like human babies, they are born instead of being hatched. (And they look like small versions of adult sharks.) Blue sharks and hammerheads are in this category.

DO SHARKS HAVE BELLY BUTTONS?

Some do.

Viviparous sharks have belly buttons when they're born, and researchers can tell how old the shark is based on how much it has healed. The state of healing also gives them an idea how big a shark was when it was born.

WHAT ARE SHARK EGGS LIKE?

Just as sharks vary, so do their eggs. Some of the eggs are laid and develop outside of the shark after they're fertilized. Others develop inside. Some eggs develop a lot like mammal eggs do—turning into embryos when they're fertilized—however, sharks developed this kind of reproduction before mammals evolved.

Shark eggs aren't shaped like chicken eggs. They range from about 4 inches to almost 10 inches in length, and they tend to be round or oval. Many develop protective cases with tendrils or hooks on their corners (they look a bit like horns). They use these to attach to plants, rocks, and other objects.

The hornshark egg case is extra-cool—it is laid on rocks and hardens into something that looks like a drill bit.

The egg contains a yolk sac that feeds the developing shark pup for up to nine months. Sometimes the egg cases are called mermaid's purses, and they wash up on the beach. Scientists in England and South Africa have asked people to report when they find shark egg casings. This tells them that adult sharks are nearby and helps with research. If you find one, maybe your discovery can be part of someone's study!

HOW OLD ARE SHARKS WHEN THEY REPRODUCE?

There are many kinds of sharks, and they have different life spans. One really important milestone, though, is when sharks are old enough to reproduce. The longer a shark takes to have offspring, the harder it is to survive long enough to reproduce—especially when humans are hunting them or damaging their habitats.

We know there is a lot to learn about this.

For example, we used to think female great white sharks were ready to reproduce when they were between 7–13 years old. We thought males had to be between 4–10.

Turns out we were very wrong.

A 2014 study that found a way to accurately determine the age of sharks discovered that great whites live a lot longer than we previously thought. Males aren't ready to reproduce until they're 26. Females take even longer—33 years.

This means that sharks are slow to replace themselves and are more vulnerable than we thought.

This is why, even though we already know some things about shark reproduction, we must learn more.

HOW MANY BABIES DO THEY HAVE AT ONCE?

The range here is huge. Sand tigers have just one or two pups at once because the rest get eaten. Blue sharks have been recorded as having as many as 134 pups in a litter. Whale sharks have carried litters of 300, but this is rare.

All shark pups are small versions of the sharks they will become, though. They're fully formed when hatched or born.

EGGS FOR BREAKFAST?

Growing sharks need food. The bigger and better fed they are, the more likely they are to survive the perils of the sea (which include being swallowed by a larger shark).

Some sharks produce extra eggs for this purpose. Unfertilized eggs are released into the uterus for the growing sharks to eat. This is called oophagy. (It's pronounced oh-OFF-a-gee.)

Bigeye threshers, shortfin mako, and porbeagle sharks do this. These unfertilized eggs are released after the others have been fertilized.

Sometimes, though, these other eggs are fertilized, which means they could develop into sharks. Sand tiger sharks eat both infertile eggs *and* their developing brothers and sisters while gestating. There's a word for eating your sibling: *adelphophagy.*

This game of sand-tiger-shark survivor continues until there's just one shark left in each of the mother's two uteri. They're big when they're born—about three feet long.

A researcher learned the hard way how ferocious these baby sand tiger sharks can get. He put his hand into a pregnant shark's uterus, and the baby bit him.

About 14 percent of all sharks are cannibals in the womb, eating unfertilized eggs and their developing siblings.

NO DAD REQUIRED

It's not entirely true that there are three types of reproduction. Sometimes sharks reproduce all on their own, without mating at all. This is called parthenogenesis (PAR-thuh-noh-GEN-uh-sis).

For an egg to be fertilized, it needs a second set of chromosomes to develop an embryo. Sometimes, the female can provide both sets of chromosomes. This is common in insects, and it happens with some fish, some reptiles, and even turkeys.

Female sharks and rays that have been isolated from males for a long time have given birth this way in captivity. For example, a white-spotted bamboo shark female had offspring that lived for several years. It's not clear whether this also happens in the wild—but it's certainly wild to ponder.

SHARKS HAVE NURSERIES, TOO

Most species of coastal sharks set aside parts of their habitat to be used as nurseries. This is where shark eggs are laid or babies are delivered, and where the young spend the earliest parts of their lives (how long depends on the type of shark).

Usually, these nurseries are shallow, safe from predators, and rich with food.

ARE SHARKS GOOD PARENTS?

When shark pups are born, they can fend for themselves. They don't rely on their parents for food. Their parents don't have to teach them to swim or hunt or evade predators (in fact, their parents might *be* the predators).

So, sharks don't look after their offspring the way people and many other animals do. But they are successful at the first task of parenting, which is to reproduce in the first place.

A DAY IN THE LIFE

You probably have routines for your days—routines that vary depending on the season, and whether you have school and that sort of thing.

Sharks do, too. Within individual days and nights, they might cover a lot of territory, both through the ocean and up and down within it. Over seasons, they might migrate long distances, alone or in groups. Scientists would love to learn more about how sharks occupy their time and how and when and where they interact with other sharks.

It can be challenging to gather this information. Sharks can swim fast and far. They can also dive deep, where it's tough for us to go. Whatever they're doing and wherever they're going, they're trying to find food, stay alive, and reproduce.

Here are some ways they do that:

THEY HUNT AT NIGHT. Most sharks eat at night, but they'll also feed during the day. Some hunt alone. Others hunt in groups. It's not clear just how much sharks eat. Some eat every one to two days, relatively small amounts of food—about 3–5 percent of their body weight. Compare this with birds, which eat a lot more as a measure of their body weight. Warblers, for example, eat 80 percent of their weight every day.

The more we learn about sharks, the more we learn how much they eat. For example, in the 1980s, a study estimated that 66 pounds of mammal blubber could keep a shark going for more than six weeks. But a study published by the University of Tasmania in 2013 found that this amount of food would only last a shark 12–15 days. They calculated this by tagging a dozen great whites, studying how fast they were swimming, and how many calories they were burning doing it. This is what's known as the metabolic rate. To keep nourished, a shark would have to eat the equivalent of a baby seal every three days, the scientists found. That's a lot more than was previously thought.

THEY FOLLOW THEIR FOOD. Sharks migrate in part because their prey does. Birds migrate, too, depending on the season of the year. But sharks' patterns are even more complicated. They depend on how mature the sharks are and whether they are yet of breeding age, because they also travel every year or two to mating grounds and nurseries.

Scientists are tagging different species of sharks to learn more. Some research programs even involve anglers. For example, the National Oceanic and Atmospheric Administration has a program where they work with both commercial and recreational fishermen to tag sharks along the Atlantic and Gulf coasts of North America and Europe. The volunteers attach tags and mail in information about when and where the shark was tagged, how big it was, and what sex it was. When sharks with tags are caught, the same information is also recorded.

Since 1962, more than 243,000 sharks from 52 species have been tagged. More than 14,000 from 33 species have been recaptured. The data help the NOAA know how far and where sharks travel. A blue shark has nabbed the record for longest travel: 3,997 miles.

Meanwhile, a sandbar shark went 27.8 years between being tagged and recaptured.

NOAA is learning surprising things with other tagging programs. The basking shark is a large, rare shark with a huge mouth it uses to suck in plankton and tiny crustaceans called copepods. Scientists learned interesting things about basking shark routines and what influences them.

Using tags that tracked movements with a satellite, they learned that basking sharks didn't change their behavior based on the time of day, like you might. Rather, they were chasing food that is carried by ocean currents. As the copepods in particular moved, the sharks adjusted to keep up, the researchers found. In a single day, a basking shark dived more than 50 times, sometimes getting as low as 160 feet below sea level.

And the copepods, though tiny, proved to be tricky prey. If they realized too many of their neighbors were being eaten, they'd try to get away, forcing the basking sharks to respond. This is the sort of information that's very difficult to learn without the help of technology. Why? For starters, that 160-foot depth the basking shark reached is deeper than humans are generally able to dive—130 feet is often the recommended limit, although people do dive deeper.

MIGRATION IS ESSENTIAL.

Sharks travel sometimes very long distances. A female great white shark tagged in November 2003 crossed the Indian Ocean and back before her tag fell off in February 2004. This was a 12,400-mile journey, and she moved swiftly, averaging almost three miles per hour. This is the fastest long-distance speed yet recorded for a migrating shark.

Researchers learned more than her distance and speed. They also learned how deep she swam, how warm the water was, and how much light she was exposed to underwater. This is important information for people trying to protect sharks. Sharks can be kept safer by local legislation and efforts. But when they travel into international waters, they lose this protection and become vulnerable all over again. The more we know about sharks and what they need to thrive, the more effective our conservation efforts can be.

MALES AND FEMALES MIGHT NOT MIX

With some shark species, such as blue sharks and spiny dogfish, the only times males and females interact is during mating season. The rest of the time, they spend in single-sex groups. Female sharks further split into pregnant and nonpregnant groups. Young sharks stick with one another, and pups avoid the adults altogether and stay in nurseries (so they don't get eaten).

DO SHARKS PLAY?

Many animals play. Humans, for one. So do puppies, elephants, chimpanzees, bears, rats, and dolphins. Scientists aren't certain why animals do this. It takes time and energy, and sometimes, someone gets hurt. It's bad enough when you're sidelined with a broken bone or other injury. For an animal, though, that kind of thing can mean death.

So why do they do it?

Some people think the play is meant to teach young animals adult behaviors, such as hunting. This might not be quite right. One scientist who observed meerkat play found the playful ones didn't end up *better* at these skills they were supposed to be learning. Playing didn't make them less aggressive, and it didn't make them bond better with one another. Another study found that squirrels and wild horses that played were more likely to live past the age of one. And these playful squirrels had more babies, which is really important for animals. So play might contribute to survival in ways we don't yet understand.

Rats are frequently studied creatures, and it

turns out they're very playful—and it helps them in important ways. Rats who grew up with other rats and toys grow bigger, more connected brains and learn faster. It wasn't just the presence of companions and interesting objects; more play meant more rapid brain growth.

It's possible that sharks play. One study observed sharks playing tug-of-war with a ship's crew. The sharks did two unusual things, in addition to returning for more tugging on a rope tied to a bag of fish. They rolled on their backs, and they kept their eyes open as they bit the bag of fish on the rope. Rolling over is a sign of relaxation, and great whites typically roll back their eyes for protection when they are biting. Observers have also witnessed great whites using penguins as chew toys— nipping them without killing them, and they only rarely eat them. (It doesn't sound all that fun for the penguin, but that is apparently the way the bird bounces in nature.)

CAN SHARKS TALK?

We don't know much about shark communication. They're often solitary creatures and their habitat makes it challenging to observe them. They don't make noises like whales and dolphins do. This doesn't mean sharks are dummies—just that they lack vocal cords.

Scientists can make guesses about how sharks communicate, though. They've observed that sharks seem to understand what other animals around them are doing, whether they're threats or rivals for prey, and whether they are receptive to mating overtures.

There are several reasons scientists think sharks are intelligent:

THEY CAN BE TRAINED LIKE DOLPHINS AND WHALES—AND THEY CAN LEARN FROM EACH OTHER

Trainers at the Shedd Aquarium in Chicago taught sharks to respond to cues in the same way whales and dolphins do. What's more, they can teach other sharks. A 1963 study showed that lemon sharks and nurse sharks could learn to press a target with their snouts until a bell rang. (They were rewarded with food.)

It took less than a week to teach the sharks to do this, and they remembered how for weeks afterward.

In a follow-up study, sharks that hadn't been taught how to ring the food bell were paired with sharks that had. Another group was placed with other sharks that didn't know to ring the bell. The

ones that had trained sharks as partners figured out how to earn the food faster than the ones that didn't. This means they were learning from (or were taught by) other sharks.

SHARKS HAVE RELATIVELY LARGE BRAINS

If you look at a shark's brain as a percentage of its body weight, it has one of the highest brain-to-body ratios of any fish. It is nowhere near the human ratio (our brains are 25 times heavier, in comparison). But it's not a small brain for an animal, and more like a bird's or a mammal's than a typical fish's brain.

The cerebrum, which is used for learning and memory, is only the size of a walnut. The rest of the brain is substantial, though. A large part is used for processing sensory information the shark receives, especially smell—and sharks have literally killer senses, as you'll learn in Chapter 2: The Perfect Predator.

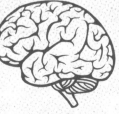

SHARK BODY LANGUAGE

Nonverbal communication is important for both humans and animals. You can sometimes tell, for example, when someone is mad at you just by looking at his or her facial expressions and posture.

There is a vast range of communication forms in nature. Think about what a dog is doing when it urinates on a shrub. It's saying, "This bush is mine." Other dogs smell this and might respond in kind. "No! It's mine!"

Fireflies and peacocks put on visual displays for each other. None of these involve language, but they're still ways to say things like, "I'm here. Look at me. Go away."

Sharks communicate with their bodies, too.

For example, two sharks might circle each other, possibly to determine which one outranks the other. Another way to establish a hierarchy is for two sharks to swim alongside each other. The lower-ranking one will swim away.

Sometimes sharks show off their sides in an attempt to intimidate another shark. Sharks will also do things like splash their tails to let other sharks know to keep away from their kill. They might also hunch their backs in response to a threat, sort of like the way a cat hisses and puffs up its fur. These are ways sharks avoid fighting each other without using language.

Mating signals are nonverbal, too. Females will move fins to indicate they're ready to mate, and they sometimes stay in shallow water if they want to avoid mating, because it's harder for the males to reach them there.

They might not use language, as some other animals do. But they have ways of communicating all the same.

SHARK MYTHS: BUSTED

MYTH: SHARKS NEVER STOP MOVING

Sharks need to breathe, and to do this, they need to move water over their gills. They can keep that water flowing by swimming, or they can suck it over their gills with the buccal muscles in their mouths.

MYTH: SHARKS DON'T NEED TO REST

It's true they don't sleep like people do. Or like male lions, which nap up to 20 hours a day. Sharks do have active and restful periods.

MYTH: SHARKS WANT TO EAT PEOPLE

On very rare occasions, sharks have bitten people. Some of those people have died (most people bitten by sharks do not die). Some incidents were provoked by humans, and others were accidents.

MYTH: ALL SHARKS HAVE SHARP TEETH

Shark teeth have evolved to be effective against sharks' prey. Some sharks don't even use their teeth to feed. The whale shark has tiny teeth, and lots of them—about 300 rows in each jaw. They don't appear to play any role in feeding.

MYTH: SHARKS DON'T GET CANCER

Sharks have powerful immune systems. Some people believe sharks don't get cancer. More improbably, some people think that certain shark body parts have magical curative powers—which is very bad news for sharks hunted for their fins and livers.

There's a lot we can learn about immune systems from understanding how sharks resist viral and bacterial infection. But they don't offer magical cures for our own diseases. And sharks do seem to get cancer, even though it's rare for us to observe. A 2013 report in *Journal of Fish Diseases* talked about lesions observed in a great white shark and a bronze whaler shark.

MYTH: SHARKS LIVE ONLY IN THE OCEAN

There are sharks in every ocean. But some sharks can survive in lagoons, which are salty pools of water separated from the ocean by sand or reefs. Some sharks can live in freshwater lakes and rivers, including bull sharks and river sharks.

MYTH: SHARKS HAVE NO ENEMIES

Many sharks are apex predators, meaning there are no animals higher on the food chain. However, experts estimate that humans kill 100 million to 200 million sharks each year. They do have an enemy, and it is us.

MYTH: SHARKS CAN SMELL A SINGLE DROP OF BLOOD IN THE OCEAN

They have a great sense of smell—as sensitive as one part per million. There are more than a million drops of water in the ocean, though. Great whites can smell small amounts of blood in the water from as far away as three miles. If they're not hungry, though, they won't even go look for the source.

MYTH: A SHARK WOULD MAKE A COOL PET

As fascinating as they are, sharks do not make good pets. Sharks like great whites, for example, are used to swimming long distances. They can't do this in aquariums. Feeding them would also be a challenge. Finally, we don't know enough about their behavior to be able to provide them with everything they need to stay healthy and happy. Some sharks do manage to survive in captivity, but many live much shorter lives because of it.

AN INTERVIEW WITH SHARK EXPERTS

Michael Heithaus and Linda Heithaus are shark researchers at Florida International University. Part of their work is focused on the importance of predators in ecosystems, and what happens when those predators disappear. When predators are killed in unprecedented numbers, as has happened with sharks, this can cause huge effects on the food chain and habitat. This is because predators are important not just for the animals they consume. A predator influences a habitat in more ways than by eating prey. Its presence changes the behavior of prey animals—behavior that can influence the environment in ways we haven't predicted or even considered. Alarmingly, in some areas, shark populations are down 90 percent or more, so it's an urgent problem to understand.

WHEN DID YOU FIRST BECOME INTERESTED IN SHARKS?

MICHAEL HEITHAUS: I have always loved the oceans, including sharks. My real interest in sharks started when I was doing my graduate research and noticed that many dolphins had scars from shark bites. I started working on sharks and have been fascinated ever since!

LINDA HEITHAUS: I first became interested in sharks when I was 10 years old. I went on my first ocean fishing trip (off Vancouver, British Columbia), and the first fish I ever caught was actually a shark (a dogfish). I was so intrigued because it didn't look like anything I had ever seen before. Little did I know it would be the first of many sharks I would see! From 10 years old, I knew I wanted to be a marine biologist.

WHAT IS YOUR FAVORITE THING ABOUT YOUR JOB?

MH: Choosing one thing is so hard, but it would have to be the privilege of being able to be so close to such amazing animals and to get to work with them. Working with great people (especially Linda) and traveling to and working in some of the most spectacular places in the world are also parts of the job that I love. But I also love sharing the results of our work—and the excitement of science—with the public, especially kids!

LH: My favorite thing about my job is seeing the animals up close. When there's a big shark on your line, it's like Christmas morning waiting to see which one it is. I also love helping kids learn all about sharks and how cool and important they are.

WHAT IS YOUR FAVORITE TYPE OF SHARK AND WHY?

MH: I really like tiger sharks. They are beautiful animals and are really important to marine ecosystems. I'm also a big fan of hammerheads—such bizarre-looking creatures.

LH: I love all sharks, but if I had to pick a favorite, it is the great hammerhead. I love their unique heads. They are surprisingly fragile yet so beautiful.

WHAT'S THE MOST INTERESTING THING YOU HAVE LEARNED ABOUT SHARKS—OR IF THERE IS ANY ONE THING YOU WISH PEOPLE KNEW ABOUT SHARKS, WHAT IS IT?

MH: For me, it is amazing just how much tiger sharks can affect their ecosystems. Over more than 15 years we have found that they affect the behavior of even species that people thought were too smart to worry about sharks, like dolphins. By scaring their prey (more than eating them) like sea turtles and sea cows, the tiger sharks actually protect large areas of sea grass from being overgrazed. That, in turn, means the sharks are protecting habitats that are important nurseries for fish and invertebrates.

CHAPTER TWO

THE PERFECT PREDATOR—

SHARKS AND THEIR ARMOR

SECRETS OF SHARK ANATOMY

When we talk about sharks, it's important to remember that they're not all great whites. There are more than 500 species organized into 34 families and 8 orders. Some researchers have even found hybrids—sharks that are mixes of more than one type.

Sharks can be found in tropical, temperate, and polar climates and in both salt and freshwater. They can live anywhere from shallow coastal environments all the way to the deep ocean. They hunt in different ways and eat all sorts of different things, though none are vegetarian. They come in all shapes and sizes. The slow-moving whale shark is the largest fish in the sea and can get up to 40 feet long. Meanwhile, a dwarf lanternshark would fit in the palm of your hand.

So when we're studying sharks and their fascinating anatomy, we'll be talking about things that are generally true for all sharks, and then zeroing in on specific features of certain sharks.

SHARKSKIN

You might have heard of something called a shark-skin suit. Don't worry—this is a woven fabric that first got popular in the 1950s. The material used for suits and napkins and such is not made from the hide of real sharks.

Some people *do* use sharkskin for decorative accents or even things like fancy boots. But the actual skin of sharks is rough. Really rough.

When the teeth are still attached, it's called sha-green and is related to the French word *chagrin*, which means "anxiety or embarrassment"—in this case, over the rough texture of the hide. And yes, some would argue that it is an embarrassment to take the skin of an incredible animal and turn it into something as mundane as a shoe, but the term is more a commentary on the roughness rather than the source.

How rough is sharkskin? Rough enough to provide the perfect nonslip covering for early Japanese sword handles. Also rough enough to be used as sandpaper. And it can really scrape softer animals that glide by it. It's both armor and a weapon, and it's a wonder, especially when it is still attached to the shark. It comes in many different colors. Gray and brown are common. It's often darker on the top and lighter on the bottom, making the sharks harder to see. This is called countershading, and it's an evolutionary advantage for many animals.

Sharkskin is usually both tough and rough, and covered in something called dermal denticles. These denticles are a lot like tiny teeth. If you look at a side view, the denticles jut out like fangs. They're covered in enamel. Like teeth, they're rooted below the skin. There's even a pulp cavity inside of them. And, like other shark teeth, most are shed continuously for as long as the shark lives. This would keep a shark tooth fairy—if there were such a thing—very busy.

In some sharks, the dermal denticles have evolved in spectacular ways. The bramble shark, for example, has thorny spines on its back. Saw sharks have long snouts edged with teeth; their snouts are called rostrums. The Mandarin shark has spines next to its dorsal fins. A weird fact about some spines: They're a bit like trees in that they develop growth rings that can sometimes be used to tell the age of a shark.

Females, especially blue sharks, often have thicker skin than males. This is to protect them during mating; sometimes the males are prone to delivering significant love bites. Whale sharks—the biggest fish in the world—have skin that is up to four inches thick.

Below the toothy layer is a mesh of tough and flexible fibers made of collagen, a protein. This is

like a natural version of chain mail, and it protects sharks from potential predators and the elements.

On the outer armor, the sharp part of the tooth points toward the shark's tail, so if you were to run your hand from back to front, you'd feel a difference. As with cat fur, it's smooth one way and rough the other.

These teeth protect the shark, but they also make it more aerodynamic underwater. Researchers studying the shortfin mako shark have observed how the creature's flexible scales help control something called flow separation. This is what happens when turbulence and differences in pressure cause drag, which can slow a shark down. The scales are flexible and can bristle outward at 60-degree angles. This helps the shark accelerate at deadly speeds—up to 60 miles per hour.

Eventually, understanding how this works might help us design faster and more efficient airplanes, helicopters, boats, and windmills. Sharkskin has already inspired the design of suits for Olympic swimmers and sailboats. For a while, the film put on boats for racing, made of a material called riblets, was banned for giving an unfair advantage. And it's not just speed the roughness of sharkskin can help us with. A company in Colorado makes shark-inspired, bacteria-resistant surface materials for hospitals, public bathrooms, and restaurant kitchens.

CAN SHARKS DARKEN?

Chris Lowe and Gwen Goodman-Lowe are shark biologists who made an interesting discovery about young scalloped hammerhead sharks: They can tan. The hammerheads were in shallow outdoor pools, and the Lowes put an opaque patch on the sharks' skin. A few days later, they removed the patches—the skin around the area was darker. Voilà! Shark tan!

It stands to reason that if sharks can tan, their skin can also burn, which is probably why they tend to stay away from the surface.

SHARK FINS

It's hard to think of a more iconic symbol of the shark than the dorsal fin, that triangular wedge that rises out of the water as the predator glides by. This blade of a shark fin slicing through waves is more of a Hollywood image than a real-life one, though. Movie directors do it because it's a lot cheaper to build a shark fin than it is to build an entire fake shark.

In real life, most sharks don't come to the surface much. Sometimes, sharks do get in water that is too shallow for their bodies and their fins poke out (and often these shallow areas are where young sharks stay safe as they grow). Tiger sharks sometimes chase sea turtles and other prey into shallow water, exposing their fins to the surface.

Some stay in that middle zone between the seafloor and surface, possibly in part because the ultraviolet rays that penetrate the top layers of the ocean can burn their skin.

Many species keep close to the bottom as a habit—it's where their food is. Some sharks even use rounded pectoral fins that look a bit like oven mitts to scoot along the bottom, and even occasionally out of the water in tide pools and on reefs.

Just as sharks vary in shape and size, so do their fins. But all sharks use their fins to help them swim. There are five types of fins, and they get their rigid structure from rods of cartilage as well as long, stiff fibers known as ceratotrichia.

DORSAL FIN

CAUDAL FIN

PELVIC FINS

PECTORAL FIN

DORSAL FIN: These stabilize the shark. What's less well-known about dorsal fins is that sharks usually have two: one near the center of their backs, and one closer to the tail. Some sharks even have protective spines before one or both of their dorsal fins.

CAUDAL FIN: This is the shark's tail fin, and it's shaped a bit like an arrow. This is the fin sharks use to propel themselves forward, and because sharks are such efficient swimmers, this tail fin is one of the most important parts of its body. In most sharks, the top half of the arrow is larger than the bottom half. The mako, a fast swimmer, has a nearly symmetrical tail. The thresher shark has a really asymmetrical tail fin.

PECTORAL FINS: These emerge from each side and, like airplane wings, produce lift. They also help a shark steer.

PELVIC FINS: These are behind the pectoral fins. They help the shark remain stable while swimming.

ANAL FIN: Not all sharks have them. They're on the shark's belly (known as the ventral side). They provide stability. So do the lateral keels of fast-swimming sharks. These aren't fins, but are a widening and flattening of the shark's sides just in front of the caudal fin.

NO BONES ABOUT IT

All living things are organized into groups of related animals. So when we talk about things like "species," that's one sort of classification, and generally describes animals that are closely related enough to produce offspring. Here's where it fits in a bigger picture:

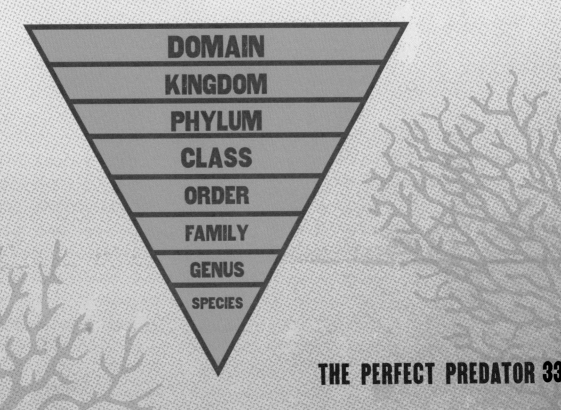

DOMAIN
KINGDOM
PHYLUM
CLASS
ORDER
FAMILY
GENUS
SPECIES

An animal's scientific name comes from its genus and species. A great white, for example, is a *Carcharodon carcharias* (it literally means "sharpened-tooth type of shark").

The various shark species belong to part of a class of animal called Chondrichthyes. Every animal in this class has a skeleton made of cartilage instead of bone. There are two main groups of cartilaginous fish, and the one that contains sharks, skates, and rays is Elasmobranchii, a word that combines "plate" (*elasmo*) and "gills" (*branchii*). (Rays are so closely related to sharks they're sometimes called pancake sharks.)

In addition to having skeletons made of cartilage instead of bones, sharks all have five to seven gill openings on each side, rigid dorsal fins, two-chambered hearts, spiracles to help breathing, skin with toothlike placoid scales, several rows of

teeth that continuously replace themselves, and upper jaws that are not fused to their skulls.

If you were to compare a shark's skeleton with that of a bony fish, it would seem simpler. Sharks have a skull, the special jaw, bony structures that support the gills, a vertebral column that runs all the way from the head to the tail, and cartilaginous structures that make the fins sturdy. Sharks don't have ribs. Out of water for long, they would be crushed by their own body weight.

The jaw and backbone need to be harder than the rest of the structural supports, so these are made of cartilage that has been hardened by calcium salts. They look like bone, but they're really light, because cartilage is only half as dense as bone. Cartilage is also flexible, which helps the shark move faster and perform tighter turns—two things that improve its ability to hunt.

THE WHOLE TOOTH AND NOTHING BUT

Shark mouths are conveyor belts of teeth. Every shark has rows and rows of teeth on their upper and lower jaws, and the new ones form in a valley behind the old and push forward as the sharks shed the old, a process that begins even before birth. Unlike our

teeth, which are rooted in our gums, shark teeth are merely embedded. This makes it easier for sharks to shed them (and it doesn't hurt, as it does when we lose a tooth).

It's hard to say how many teeth a shark will grow

and lose in its lifetime. All sharks have different teeth—in both shape and number. Also, determining the average length of a shark's life span isn't easy. Some sharks, such as the great white, don't fare well in captivity and therefore are tough to study closely. And sharks might keep their teeth for just over a week or for several months, depending on the species and season of the year. A shark might have as many as 3,000 teeth in their mouth at once (though not all sharks will have this many). It's safe to say, though, that a shark might grow and shed tens of thousands of teeth in its lifetime.

The variety of teeth is astonishing. Some are microscopic. Some are pointed. Some are flatter and used to crush shellfish. Some curve. Some have serrated edges. Some are spear-shaped, all the better to impale tiny swimming prey. All are evolved to help the shark survive.

Shark teeth resist cavities for a couple of reasons. For starters, they don't keep them for long. Also, shark tooth enamel is covered with fluorapatite, a chemical that resists the tooth-rotting acid produced by bacteria in the mouth.

DO SHARKS CHEW?

Sharks typically use their teeth to seize prey, hold it, and rip off bites. They also crush prey. But they don't chew.

Some sharks eat plankton, and these sharks have fewer teeth and instead rely on filters. Whale sharks do this, vacuuming water into their mouths at a high speed as they hover in the water. Filtering pads cover the entrance of their throats, and these have millimeter-wide pores that trap food particles but let water pass through. They expel the water

through their gills, keeping the food in their mouths. Sometimes food gets stuck in the whale shark's gills, and scientists think the sharks cough to get rid of it. Amazingly enough, eating mostly plankton (along with some small crustaceans, squid, and larger plants), whale sharks eat enough to become the largest fish in the world.

One fascinating bit about shark teeth: They're really scales that have evolved to help sharks hunt and feed. Like our teeth, they have a hole in the middle filled with pulp. A dentine layer covers this. The teeth are capped with a protective enamel layer. The crown of a shark's tooth develops first, inside the inner jaw.

HOW DO SHARK TEETH BECOME FOSSILS?

There are even some well-preserved teeth of extinct sharks, thanks in part to the teeth's incredible hardness. Intact teeth of the enormous megatooth shark—*Carcharodon megalodon*—have been found, even though this creature is believed to have died out 4 million years ago. These teeth provide clues to how and where they fed, mated, and migrated. Ancient shark teeth have also been found in surprising places, including a cache of more than 8,000 discovered in Banks Island, Canada, which today is a frozen and barren land. The teeth are believed to have been deposited there in the Eocene epoch, 38–53 million years ago, according to a study published in the November 2014 issue of the *Journal of Vertebrate Paleontology*.

It takes a long time for a tooth to turn into a fossil. The ones that survived to become fossils fell to the seafloor and were buried quickly. The sediment protected the teeth from exposure to water, currents, and scavengers, as well as oxygen and bacteria that would cause decay. Then, over a period of thousands of years, water seeped through the buried treasures and filled the pores of teeth with minerals, which hardened. These minerals change the original color of the teeth, so you might come across ones that are blue-gray, black, reddish-orange, white, or even green ones—but it doesn't mean the shark originally had a Technicolor smile.

Fossils can provide all sorts of clues about how sharks live. They've even definitely proved that young megalodon from the late Miocene grew up in nurseries—10 million years after the fact.

SMILE!

The goblin shark has a mouth full of skinny, curved teeth below a protruding snout. It gets our vote as the shark with the weirdest teeth.

HOW TO IDENTIFY SHARKS BY THEIR TEETH

It can be tricky to identify sharks by their teeth. Sometimes males and females of the same species have different teeth. Sharks can also be hard on their teeth, which can end up chipped, cracked, or misshapen. And many species have teeth so similar it's hard to tell them apart.

But there are a handful of clues you can use to distinguish them:

FOSSIL SHARKS

Paleontologists use three things to tell one fossil tooth from another: shape, serration, and root shape.

IS THE TOOTH TRIANGULAR, LIKE A TORTILLA CHIP?

Or is it slender and pointy, more like a nail? Sandtiger sharks have skinny, pointed teeth. Megalodon teeth are triangular. Scientists also study whether the tooth is hooked or straight, and whether the top and bottom teeth are the same or different.

IS THE TOOTH SERRATED OR SMOOTH?

The Otodus shark has a very smooth tooth. Extinct species of weasel sharks have teeth like jagged steak knives. Paleontologists count serrations, measure them, and determine if they cover the whole tooth or only part. A dusky shark, for example, has big serrations at the base of the tooth, but taper to almost nothing at the tip.

WHAT SHAPE AND SIZE ARE THE ROOTS?

Some are lobed. Some are shallow. Sometimes the root is deep. Scientists also look at how the width of the root compares with the length of the "blade" of the tooth. Some ancient tiger sharks have a tooth blade that's twice as long as the root is wide, for example, while the Squalicorax teeth have fat roots. In some sharks, roots have notches. The way the blade of the shark tooth connects to its roots can also tell you what kind of shark tooth it is. Great white sharks, for example, have a thin seam between the blade and the root.

COLOR OFTEN DOESN'T MATTER.

Different minerals and different amounts of oxygen can make one fossil tooth have a different color from a different fossilized tooth of the same species of shark. This is why color won't tell you anything about the species. But color can tell if a tooth is modern or ancient. Typically, a tooth from a living shark is going to be closer to white.

LIVING SPECIES OF SHARKS

Scientists still consider tooth shape, serration, and root shape to identify the teeth of modern sharks. Generally, teeth aren't the best way to identify sharks, though, because many different species have very similar teeth.

Still, there are some questions you can ask yourself:

IS THE TOOTH DEEPLY NOTCHED?
Some shark teeth are curved. The space behind the curve is called the notch. Some shark teeth have very deep notches. The sixgill shark is one of these. In contrast, a lemon shark's teeth are thin, pointy, and straight.

ARE THERE ANY GIVEAWAY IDENTIFIERS?
Some shark teeth are unique, and when you see them, you know exactly what kind of shark it is. For example, the modern sandtiger shark has evolved two tiny extra daggers on either side of the main tooth blade.

SHARK SENSES:
COMMON AND UNCOMMON

THE DANCE OF SENSES

When they hunt, sharks use all their senses, but not necessarily all at once. Smell and hearing work over the longest distances. Moving in closer to their targets, sharks depend on vision and something called a lateral line, which detects motion. At very close range, sharks use organs called the ampullae of Lorenzini to determine exactly where the prey is and to orient their jaws for attack. And last comes taste, which is why sometimes sharks bite humans and swim away— we don't taste like prey.

We don't know everything we can about these complex senses in sharks. But we are learning all the time. Researchers trying to understand more about how sharks use their senses when hunting conducted experiments meant to block one sense at a time, for example.

In one experiment, they plugged the sharks' noses with cotton soaked in petroleum jelly. Blacktip sharks and bonnetheads found the prey even without being able to smell it, but nurse sharks didn't, which told the scientists that nurse sharks rely on this sense in the wild (even though they can be trained to rely more on sight in captivity). Nurse sharks could find prey without seeing it. These differences between species are probably due to the fact that each shark hunts differently in the wild, and different senses are useful in different ways.

Here's more about each sense and what we know about how they work:

THE EYES HAVE IT

We used to think that sharks had lousy eyesight and made up for this with heightened senses elsewhere. Now we know this isn't the case. Their eyesight is as well adapted to their environments as their other senses—and in clear water, they might see 10 times as much light as we do, giving them an edge.

In many ways, though, their eyes are like human ones. They have rods, which let them detect light and darkness, and cones, which let them see color. They also have corneas, lenses, retinas, pupils, and irises—just like us.

Unlike humans (but like many nocturnal animals), sharks have something called a tapetum lucidum. This is a layer of mirrored crystals behind the retina, and it bounces light back toward the retina again, as sort of a second chance for vision. Animals that have this can see better in the dark (even if things are a bit blurrier). This is how sharks improve their vision in murky water.

Sharks have eyelids, but these don't work like ours. Some also have a clear nictitating membrane that slides and protects the eye when the shark is biting. These membranes are common—even dogs and cats have them, but you usually can't see them unless you gently open their eyes while they're sleeping. Great whites don't have this, so they roll their pupils back in their heads when feeding.

Interestingly, the size of a shark's eyes depends on how deep in the ocean it lives. The sharks living within 1,000 meters of the top, known as the pelagic and upper mesopelagic layers, are exposed to the most light and have the largest eyes. In the next layer down, the bathypelagic zone, which is 1,000–4,000 meters below the surface, sharks have smaller eyes with larger pupils, which let in more light and let them detect bioluminescence.

Sharks can also dilate their pupils to respond to levels of light, something most fish can't do. They can also keep their eyeballs warm (and vision sharp enough for hunting) in cold water using a special organ next to a muscle by the eye socket.

THE NOSE KNOWS

Sharks have nostril-like openings called nares. Unlike humans, they don't use these for breathing. They have gills for that. They use their noses entirely for smelling—detecting both prey and potential mates—and it's a powerful sense. Each nasal cavity has two openings, one for water to enter, and the other for water to leave.

You might have heard sharks can smell tiny amounts of blood in the water, and this is true. Their noses are much more sensitive than ours. The sensitivity of different sharks varies, but some are able to detect the equivalent of a single drop to a single teaspoon of blood in an Olympic-size swimming pool.

How do those extraordinary noses work?

Sharks suck in water through their nares. Water travels into the nasal sacs and over some skin folds that are called olfactory lamellae. The insides of these cavities are paved with cells, and as water flows through a shark's snout, these olfactory cells detect chemicals that have dissolved into the water. Receptors in these cells send the brain signals, and then the olfactory lobes in the shark's brain let the shark know when prey or partners are within a few thousand feet.

The majority of a shark's brain—two-thirds—is given over to detecting and evaluating scents. That's how important smell is for a shark.

HEAR, HEAR

Sharks don't have ears that stick out of their heads like human ears do, but this doesn't mean their hearing is dull. Holes on the sides of their heads lead to inner ears that can pick up sound from as far as 800 feet away. Sound travels farther and faster underwater than it does on land, so it might even be a shark's first clue that a meal is near. They hear low sounds better than high sounds.

Each shark ear contains a trio of semicircular canals, and each of these contains four sensory maculae, which are patches of hair cells that pick up vibrations. These maculae not only help sharks hear, they help them with their sense of balance.

Sharks also have something called a lateral line system. Most fish have these, and they use them to detect vibrations in the water. The lateral line runs from the shark's brain to its tail, and is a canal filled with fluid. Tiny hairs lining the walls of the lateral line sway when there are vibrations and movements. The vibrations send messages to the brain using nerve cells, telling sharks what might be nearby—and where. Human ears have an ear cochlea that contains what some call a descendant of the lateral line.

THE PLACE FOR TASTE

Of all the senses in a shark, the sense of taste is the weakest one. It makes sense. You first must find prey—you don't taste first.

Sharks have tongues, but they're not like ours. Called basihyals, shark tongues are small and thick. They're made of cartilage and rooted to the bottom of the mouths of sharks and other fishes. Most sharks don't seem to use their tongues, although the cookiecutter shark is an exception. A shark's taste buds line its mouth and throat, and these help a shark decide whether prey is to be eaten or spit out. These taste buds send signals to their brain.

When they're testing something for food potential, sharks often give a trial bite (kind of the way people do when they're trying something new for the first time). Sharks are picky and will spit out food they don't like (except for tiger sharks, which even eat tires). This is why humans bitten by sharks often survive. The bites were accidental or exploratory, and the shark moved on to more suitable food.

Sharp-eyed researchers noticed that 9 percent of California sea otters that washed up on shore had great white tooth marks on them. But they've never found sea otter remains in the stomach of a great white. What's the theory? Well, sea otters are related to skunks and weasels—stinky creatures. Maybe otters taste bad to sharks.

If sharks have something in their stomachs that really doesn't belong in there—bones, mucus, parasites, indigestible things—they can actually barf out their stomachs and then suck them back in. It's called voluntary gastric eversion, and it's a quick process that is gross to watch, but not deadly for a shark. (It's kind of like turning a tote bag inside out to remove all the pesky debris at the bottom.)

SHARKS' SIXTH SENSE

For centuries, we've been aware of the presence of small black pits covering the snouts of sharks. Italian Marcello Malpighi observed them in 1662, and his countryman Stefano Lorenzini described them more fully 16 years later, which is why these "ampullae of Lorenzini" bear his name.

The pits, which look a little bit like beard stubble, lead to gel-filled transparent tubes, Lorenzini noted. Some were small. Others were spaghetti width. The tubes traveled to the shark's head and congregated in what looked like masses of a clear jelly. But what did the pits do? Did they sense pressure? Temperature?

For centuries, the hunt was on. By the middle of the nineteenth century, researchers knew these tubes were some sort of sensory organ and were similar to the lateral line. By the early twentieth century, we learned they were sensitive to touch. Then, in 1938, a researcher found they could detect temperature changes. By the 1950s, scientists realized these organs could do something remarkable: perceive electricity.

Before then, we hadn't known animals could do this. By the 1990s, we'd learned that many aquatic animals can sense electricity. The ability to perceive the electrical field given off by a fish is important to the shark, because this sense works even when conditions for other senses are poor.

This sense is extraordinarily sharp in sharks. One researcher determined that sharks can detect the equivalent of an AA battery dipped in Long Island Sound connected to another as far away as Jacksonville, Florida. This means a shark swimming between those two points could tell whether the battery was switched on. Human engineers have a tough time measuring such a weak charge in the water even using the best equipment available.

These ampullae remain a subject of study today, with researchers pondering how these cells work and whether the ancestors of vertebrates could also detect electrical fields before they evolved to live on land.

THE THRILL OF THE GILL

Sharks breathe through their gills, which are a lot like human lungs. Sharks can have anywhere from five to seven of these slits on each side of the head, as well as a modified gill opening called a spiracle, which sits behind the shark's eye. One difference between sharks and most other fish: shark gills are uncovered. On fish gills, the covering is called an operculum.

When water flows over the gill's membranes, small blood vessels called capillaries pull oxygen

from the water. Muscles need this oxygen-rich blood to function. Once the blood has delivered oxygen to the shark's muscles, it flows through the shark's heart and back through the gills, which release carbon dioxide waste back into the water.

You might have heard that sharks need to keep moving to stay alive. This isn't quite right. They need to keep the *water* moving to stay alive, and different sharks have different ways of doing that.

Sharks that don't do much swimming have mouth muscles that pull water into the mouth and over their gills. These buccal muscles make it possible for the shark to stay still and still keep their ability to breathe. They can even do this if they're hiding under the sand, using the special breathing holes behind their eyes called spiracles.

Sharks that are strong swimmers cruise along with their mouths open, "ramming" water over their gills. Mako, great white, and whale sharks must keep swimming to breathe. Other sharks can both ram ventilate and buccal breathe. The tiger shark is one of these.

Sharks live in a challenging environment. It can be both salty and cold. Not only do shark gills help them retain heat, they can help them get rid of excess salt, which is excreted across their gills. They also have a special gland that helps them excrete the excess salt from their guts.

This adaptation means that most sharks can't tolerate freshwater. Bull sharks are an exception. They can go from salty water to freshwater rivers and lakes. They handle the change with their kidneys, which pee out some of the excess chemical waste. And they also absorb salt with their gills instead of excreting it as they would in the salty sea.

HOW SHARKS HUNT

SMELL-O-VISION

Imagine you're waving your hand through steam from a shower. The waving motion would displace the fog. This is a bit like the way sharks use scent not only to smell prey, but discern its shape and location.

Here's how it works:

A shark's lateral line detects the faint vibration of other living creatures. But it's not just picking up the vibrations. It's creating something of a 3-D model of the odor source. The scent travels in a plume, and sharks can tell when an object is disrupting it. (And many animals use these plumes to find food, mates, and shelter.)

Researchers conducted an experiment in which they squirted the scent of squid in a circulating water tank. The shark couldn't find the source until they put a brick behind it. The brick interrupted the flow of the scent, and the sharks tracked the prey.

This is another reason to be concerned about pollution in the ocean, by the way. Chemical pollution is hard on a shark's eyes and nose. Heavy metal pollutants and antibiotics can impede a shark's lateral line system.

SPECIALIZED HUNTING SYSTEMS

Even though some sharks will eat just about anything (or at least try a bite), and many sharks will eat many kinds of food, other types of sharks are more specialized. Their hunting and feeding styles have evolved accordingly.

There are four basic feeding styles:

AMBUSH HUNTING **SOLO HUNTING**
COOPERATIVE HUNTING **PLANKTON FEEDING**

AMBUSH HUNTING: Some types of sharks live camouflaged on the seafloor. These sharks lie in wait for prey to pass. Then they suck it into their mouths. A lot of ambush hunters eat only creatures with hard shells—mollusks and crustaceans. So their teeth are big and flat, like molars.

SOLO HUNTING: Certain sharks have developed rather specialized feeding systems as they hunt down their prey. The thresher shark has a caudal tail with a huge top lobe. It smacks fishes, stunning them. Then it eats them. Sawsharks use their bladed rostra like swords, slashing prey. They also use them like spoons, stirring up food resting on the seafloor. The viper shark, meanwhile, can point its fangs outward, catch prey, and swallow it whole.

Great whites and other sharks that eat large animals take a more cautious approach. They circle their prey and wait for the right moment for a swift attack. Sometimes, one bite is all it takes to kill an animal as large as a sea lion. The great white waits for it to die of blood loss and then finishes it off.

But they're not merely stealth attackers taking advantage of opportunity. They're tremendously athletic. Film footage shows great whites leaping entirely out of water as they gulp prey whole. It's breathtaking.

COOPERATIVE HUNTING: Just as land animals like spotted hyenas and lions hunt in packs, some sea creatures do this as well, including dolphins and certain species of shark. Whitetip reef sharks are an example of pack hunters. They can herd and catch prey larger than themselves. They also migrate long distances, most likely in search of food.

PLANKTON FEEDING: Just as whales can get very large by feeding on tiny plankton, so can certain kinds of sharks. Some, like the whale shark, use suction to vacuum up food. Megamouths are suction feeders. But they add luminous tissue inside of their gargantuan mouths to lure prey. Others swim with their mouths open, a behavior called ram feeding. Sharks that feed on plankton have gill rakers that act as sieves to filter water from their food.

OTHER WONDERFUL AND WEIRD TEETH

The megalodon is extinct, but its teeth will live on in the history books. They were huge. If you include the root, the teeth could measure up to seven inches long.

The largest teeth we know of belonged to the *Livyatan melvillei*, an extinct whalelike creature that had chompers as long as 14 inches.

Not all teeth are used for eating. Elephants use their tusks for foraging food and water. The tusks also make them targets for poachers, unfortunately.

Walruses drag themselves out of water with their tusks. Both males and females have them, and the tusks can grow up to three feet long. Males use them to defend their turf and offspring in mating and reproduction season.

The narwhal is a toothed whale. Males grow what look like unicorn horns that can be eight and a half feet long. But they aren't horns. They're actually the narwhal's left canine tooth, and it penetrates the male's upper lip. These freaky teeth don't have enamel, and they're used as sensory organs. Seawater penetrates the tooth through cementum channels (human teeth also have these pores). The water travels through the narwhal's tooth and send signals through the nerves there. The nerves let the animal know how cold the water is and what's in it—ranging from food to females who are ready to mate.

WHICH SHARK HAS THE MOST TEETH?

It depends on how you look at it. Are we talking teeth at any one time? Or teeth over a lifetime?

The megalodon might have had about 276 teeth at any given time, arranged in rows.

A great white might have 60 to 70 at a time.

Bull sharks have 50 rows of teeth, which they shed constantly.

Over a lifetime, the toothiest sharks might grow and shed 30,000 teeth.

LOOK SHARP, NOW

It's tough to say which shark has the sharpest teeth. But tiger sharks have teeth unlike many other sharks. They have rows of 24 top and bottom teeth with serrated edges that cut and saw prey. Usually other sharks. They also have square rather than round jaws that meet in the middle of their snout at a nearly right angle.

But their teeth still aren't as sharp as those of an extinct eel known as a condont. These died out 200 million years ago. The teeth are tiny (as was the condont, which topped out at two inches). You can't see them without a microscope. But the animal didn't have a sturdy jawbone or strong jaw muscles, so it developed sharp teeth to compensate.

SNAIL TEETH

Not all tooth-filled animals inspire terror.

Shel Silverstein once wrote a poem describing a sharp-toothed snail that lives inside your nostril and could potentially bite off a gold-digging finger. The poem is fictional, but it is true that snails have teeth—and lots of them.

A garden snail might have 14,000.

And a limpet, which is a sort of sea-dwelling snail that uses its tiny sharp teeth to scrape algae from rocks, might have teeth made of the strongest substance to be discovered by humans. Limpet teeth grow on a tonguelike structure called a radula. The teeth are less than a millimeter long. A scientist used a technique called atomic force microscopy to pull apart a sliver of this material, and a slice 100 times thinner than a human hair was stronger than spider silk, which scientists had previously thought was nature's mightiest substance.

CHAPTER THREE

STRANGE & WONDERFUL SHARKS

Sharks come in a stunning variety of shapes and sizes. And while familiar sharks such as the great white are thrilling to watch and think about, there are other sharks that inspire wonder and awe. Some are huge. Some tiny. Some so strange looking they seem like fairy-tale monsters.

All living things are organized into categories of related living things. We mentioned earlier that sharks are in a class called Chondrichthyes.

This class contains two orders: Squatiniformes and Pristiophoriformes. Each of these two orders contains families, and then is further divided into genus and species. So, while our collection of weird sharks is about species, it's useful to know what families and orders they belong to.

Squatiniformes have fewer families and species. These sharks have flattened bodies or saw-shaped noses. Then there are Pristiophoriformes. These don't have flattened bodies. There are many families of them, and as you study how they look, you can see the relationships between them. They might not be the same species, but they share characteristics.

A FEW OF THE MOST UNUSUAL SHARKS IN THE SEA:

DWARF LANTERNSHARK—*ETMOPTERUS PERRYI*

This is the smallest-known shark. It could nestle easily in an adult's hand. You're not likely to see or hold one yourself, though. It's an extremely rare little shark. The only times sightings have been recorded are off the northern tip of South America. These sharks often keep to the deep, ranging from 929–1,440 feet below the surface.

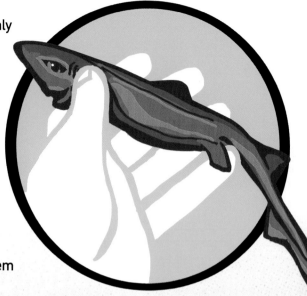

They have big eyes and their mouths curve up so it looks as though they're grinning. More spectacularly, they have organs on their belly and fins called photophores. These glow in the dark. When they're deep underwater, the light their photophores emit attracts smaller fish, which the dwarf lanternshark eats. In shallower water, their glowing bellies look like sunlight piercing the surface, protecting them from being eaten.

There's another kind of illumination lanternsharks use to foil predators from above. Some have glowing spines on their backs. Researchers from Belgium observed a larger species of lanternshark plucked from the cold waters of Norway's fjords. These two-foot-long sharks would flip and try to stab potential predators with the glowing spines on their backs.

POCKET SHARK—MOLLISQUAMA PARINI

This shark is so rare that only two sightings have been reported—both really far away from each other. It's pocket-size, but that's not where it gets its common name. This diminutive creature also has a teeny pocket in front of its pectoral fin. No one is certain what it uses the pocket for.

Since the first was found in 1984, scientists have hypothesized a few things: that it secretes chemicals that attract prey or mates, or help the shark avoid predators. The chemicals might even glow in the dark. The two pocket sharks that have been found had physical differences between them.

The first, found in the southeast Pacific Ocean, about 1,200 miles west of the coast of Chile, didn't have light-emitting organs on its belly. The second, which did, was found in 2010 in the Gulf of Mexico and identified five years later by a scientist in Mississippi's NOAA laboratory.

The differences could mean they're different species. The first was female and the second, male. The first was adult and the second young. So, it could also have to do with age or sex. Both were dark brown with rounded snouts—they look a bit like miniature whales.

BASKING SHARK—CETORHINUS MAXIMUS

After the whale shark, this is the second-largest living fish in the world, and you can find it globally in cold-to-temperate waters, in coastal habitats. They do go offshore sometimes, and also will enter bays

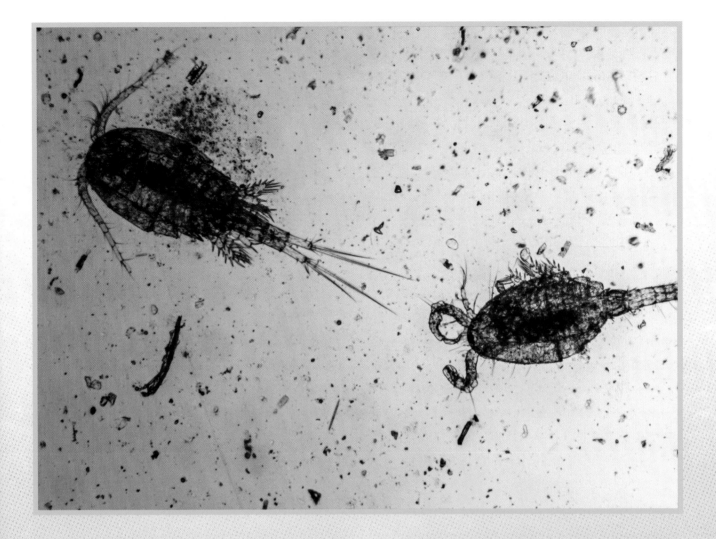

and estuaries. They're called basking sharks because of the way they sometimes appear to bask on the surface of the ocean, sucking in cope-pods and shrimp. They also dive deep—up to 1,000 meters, according to data gathered by satellite tags.

Also called sunfish and sailfish, basking sharks have absolutely enormous mouths. If you've ever put your mouth against a window and blown all your air out so your lips get stretched out and funny look-ing, then you know what a basking shark's giant maw looks like. (Its scientific name, by the way, is a combination of Greek and Latin words that mean "great marine monster nose.") Their mouths are so big, you can see their gill rakers, which look a bit like the arches of a Gothic cathedral.

They're one of three species of sharks that eat plankton, in addition to the whale shark and the megamouth. As they swim slowly, their gill rakers catch plankton in the water that's flowing in their mouths and over their gills.

Their teeth aren't what you think of when you think of shark teeth: they're tiny, with as many as 100 per row, and cone shaped with pointed tips that curve backward.

The average adult basking shark is between 22–29 feet long, but specimens as long as 40 feet have been seen.

Classified as endangered in some areas they inhabit, basking sharks take a long time to reproduce. Gestation takes an estimated one to three years. They take a year off between births, which means there is as long as a four-year gap between litters. This matters, because the slower endangered animals like the basking shark reproduce, the more vulnerable they are, and the harder it is to return their numbers to healthy amounts.

They're aplacental viviparous reproducers, and the embryos feed on unfertilized eggs before they're hatched inside their mothers' uteruses. In the 1940s, a Norwegian fisherman caught a pregnant female. She gave birth to five live sharks and one stillborn one. They were big—between about five and six and a half feet each. No shark is known to deliver larger pups.

GREAT HAMMERHEAD—*SPHYRNA MOKARRAN*

There are nine different species of hammerhead, a shark that looks as if George Lucas designed it for an underwater cantina scene. The great hammerhead is the largest of these, growing up to 20 feet long and 1,000 pounds. (Most hammerheads are a lot smaller.) Their dorsal fins are pointed and tall, making them instantly recognizable.

With white bellies and light-gray to gray-brown backs, great hammerheads live all around the world in tropical seas, along coasts, continental shelves, and reefs, and up to 80 miles offshore.

Their heads are a marvel, with wide-set eyes nestled into either end of what looks like a mallet.

This oddity gives them better vision than most sharks. A group of sensory organs called the ampullae of Lorenzini is spread across the snout. They use these to detect electrical fields given off by prey—and they're so sensitive, they can even find stingrays hiding under the sand.

They pin the stingrays with their head mallets during attacks.

One spectacular feature about this species is that they migrate in masses during the summer in search of cooler water. These hammerhead groups are called shoals or schools.

SIXGILL SAWSHARK—*PLIOTREMA WARRENI*

Sawsharks are surprising creatures. Their snouts stretch out into a rostrum—a tooth-studded growth that looks remarkably like a saw. A pair of sensory organs called barbels hangs down from the saw, looking a bit like a droopy mustache. Their teeth are supersharp, though sawsharks are no threat to humans.

All sawsharks but one have five pairs of gill slits, which makes the sixgill an oddity. Its barbels also hang closer to their mouths than those of other sawsharks, increasing the resemblance to a Fu Manchu mustache. The sawshark's rostrum comes in handy when it's hunting small fish, crustaceans, and squid. It's full of sensors to pick up the vibrations and electrical fields of prey, and is believed by experts to use these for attack and self-defense. (Foes probably include the much larger tiger shark.)

Sixgill sawsharks are small. The females are about three and a half feet long, while the males are less than three feet. They eat little fish, squid, and crustaceans. Their litters of five to seven pups hatch inside the mother.

They're found in South Africa and southeast Madagascar, preferring to inhabit near the bottom, on offshore continental shelves and upper slopes. They're a near-threatened species, often caught by fishermen and thrown away because they're not considered valuable.

MEGAMOUTH—*MEGACHASMA PELAGIOS*

These sharks, which eat plankton with their enormous mouths, are extremely rare. The species was first identified in 1976, when a US Navy research ship found one near Oahu, one of the Hawaiian Islands.

The shark was tangled in one of two parachutes the navy had been using as an anchor. They knew the 14-foot-long creature was unusual as they were pulling it out of the water by its tail using a winch. The shark's tail fin broke off, and the shark plunged back into the ocean, where divers retrieved it.

There have been fewer than 70 sightings of these sharks since.

They're large—bigger than great whites, but smaller than whale sharks and basking sharks. Their scientific names means "giant cave" in Greek, and this is a good description of the enormous mouth on these animals.

They live in the deep ocean during the day, while they rise from around 1,500 feet to a mere 50 feet from the surface at night, possibly to gulp their microscopic prey. They have been spotted in the Indian, Atlantic, and Pacific Oceans, but despite their range, they're almost never seen by humans. They're too rare to be harvested regularly by fishermen—and so difficult to find that scientists don't know whether they're endangered.

Megamouths are a bit sausage shaped. Their short, rounded snouts open with a massive mouth fringed with short teeth arranged in about 50 rows on each jaw (only three rows of them work). Females reach at least 17 feet, while males are a bit smaller, around 13 feet in length.

They're not great swimmers, probably due to the fact that their skeleton is on the soft side, as is their skin. Their muscles and connective tissue are loose, too. No one knows for sure how they eat, but scientists think megamouths swim openmouthed through schools of krill, jellyfish, plankton, and other tiny prey. They stick out their jaws and expand their mouths as much as possible to suck prey inside, and then they close their mouths and pull back their jaws, which pump excess water through their five pairs of gills.

Researchers in Indonesia once watched sperm whales surround a megamouth—and it looked like an attack. Sperm whales are thought to feed on squid, but it's possible whales might eat the sharks. They also could have just been curious, or attempting to play.

Megamouths do get attacked by cookiecutter sharks, little dogfish that have a distinctive round bite. (See page 56 for more on these creatures.)

THRESHER SHARK—ALOPIAS VULPINUS

Thresher sharks use their elegant tails as weapons. The upper lobe of a thresher shark's tail fin can be as long as their bodies, and they whip them through the water at such high speeds that they stun or kill small fish, which they then eat. Thresher sharks sometimes even hunt in groups.

Scientists think the tail slapping is a more efficient way to hunt than chasing down one fish at a time. Orcas and dolphins also hunt this way, but not quite like the thresher shark.

These tail slaps are really powerful—video shows they might be strong enough to create

underwater shock waves. That's a term that describes something moving faster than the speed of sound. These tail slaps can even be powerful enough to break down water molecules, which are two parts hydrogen and one part oxygen, into their elements. Their evidence of this is the presence of underwater bubbles formed when the slaps split the water molecules into two gases.

These sharks can be found around the world in coastal habitats, in waters ranging from somewhat cold to tropical. Their eggs hatch inside the mother, and they give birth to an average of four pups at a time.

Thresher sharks are considered shy and harmless to humans (although they've been known to attack boats). The reverse is not the case. These sharks are prized for their meat, hides, and the oil in their livers, which is turned into vitamins.

FRILLED SHARK—*CHLAMYDOSELACHUS ANGUINEUS*

For a shark that is harmless to humans, the frilled shark looks a bit like the stuff of scary movies. And it might just be the very creature that inspired ancient myths and legends about sea serpents.

The frilled shark is a long and slithery creature with a short snout that curves into a mysterious-looking grin. Bouquets of razor-sharp teeth grow

inside this mouth, which opens wide enough to accommodate prey half the length of the frilled shark's bendy body. These teeth are arranged in 25 rows, about 300 in all. Frilled sharks are a bit like snakes in the way they can gulp relatively enormous prey and digest it slowly.

This is an ancient species, probably in existence

for 80 million years. They're found around the world in patches, preferring waters 165 to almost 5,000 feet deep, where they eat squid and deepwater fish.

They're near threatened because of the way they're caught in fishermen's nets, and they reproduce slowly. It might take two years for a pregnant female to gestate her very large eggs (they're more than four inches long to start with). Litters might run anywhere from six to twelve pups, which are hatched inside the mother and swim out. They're about 15 inches long when they're born, and can grow to be about four to six and a half feet long, with the females being a bit larger than the males.

COOKIECUTTER SHARK—*ISISTIUS BRASILIENSIS*

This is the only shark that's also a parasite—an organism that hurts but doesn't necessarily kill its prey. They're tiny, one of the world's smallest sharks (about the size of a house cat), and they live in deep, tropical waters around the world, rising to the surface at night to feed.

These are strange-looking sharks. Once called the cigar shark for their shape, they have teardrop-shaped eyes and a mouth that appears to be ringed in thick lips. Their lower teeth are big, triangular, and pointy, sort of like cat teeth in a child's drawing. They also glow green in the dark, thanks to bioluminescent organs on their bellies. This is where the *Isistius* in their name comes from—Isis, the Egyptian goddess of light. (The *brasiliensis* part is because they're found off Brazil's coast.)

These glowing green organs, called photophores, help them lure prey. Any animal swimming beneath it might be tricked into thinking that there are fish above. And that's when this pint-size parasite strikes—and from where it gets its name. Its unique lips provide suction that helps it hang on to its prey. It has sharp upper teeth for the same reason. Once it has a hold of its victim, it spins its body around and slices out a round plug of meat. This leaves its victims with a round hole—and these cookie-shaped bites are often found in marlin, dolphins, tuna, squid, sharks, seals, whales, dolphins, and stingrays.

The shark has also been known to take bites out of the rubber covers on the sonar domes of nuclear submarines, as well as out of electrical cables. Sometimes, the subs have even been temporarily disabled by these bites. (Possibly the same has happened to the sharks.)

GOBLIN SHARK—*MITSUKURINA OWSTONI*

It's hard to imagine a stranger-looking creature than the goblin shark, which has a long, broad, curved nose that projects far past a grinning mouth of sharp, widely spaced teeth. Its head takes up a large percentage of its flabby, pinkish body, which is tipped with bluish fins.

As sharks go, they don't have a great deal of teeth: 26 on the top jaw, and 24 on the lower. But these are distinctive. They're skinny, long, and sharply pointed in front, and designed to crush prey in the back.

Goblin sharks can get fairly large—as long as 12 feet for both males and females. Their huge snouts are covered with ampullae of Lorenzini, making them extra sensitive to electromagnetic energy given off by prey. Their jaws are also evolved to make them swift hunters. Their jaw joints have a double set of ligaments. These are held tightly closed when the shark is swimming. When attacking, the shark relaxes the jaw, which shoots forward to snag prey and yank it back into the waiting mouth.

It is believed that goblin sharks eat shrimp, octopus, fish, squid, and crabs. No one is certain how they reproduce. No pregnant females have been captured. But they're likely to be aplacental viviparous.

JAPANESE WOBBEGONG—*ORECTOLOBUS JAPONICUS*

Sharks are an ancient life-form, but some species evolved more recently. One of those is the wobbegong (rhymes with *hop along*). They evolved around 2 million years ago. There are seven different species of wobbegong and they live in the western Pacific, from Australia to Japan.

This is one of the few sharks that can withstand life in an aquarium. In the wild, Japanese wobbegongs live near Australia, in shallow reefs. Like the rest of the wobbegongs, the Japanese version is flattened and its skin is patterned to hide it as it lurks on the sea bottom awaiting prey.

These sharks are shaped a bit like zeppelins—they're definitely not built for speed. They have broad, flat heads and heavy jaws bearing two rows of fangs on the top, and three rows on the bottom. Their skin looks a bit as though it's patterned with flowers. They have light blotches with dark edges, and a fringe of long, branched barbels hang from their snouts. They use these whiskery organs to find prey, which they suck into their mouths and impale on their sharp teeth.

Their paired pectoral fins look a bit like Ping-Pong paddles, and they use these to scoot around

the seafloor—and sometimes take short trips out of the water. You definitely don't want to step on one. They've been known to bite unwary divers, though they're far too small to be lethal to humans.

These sharks hatch inside their mothers, alongside litters of 20 or more pups at a time. They're around eight inches at birth, and grow to around three to three and a half feet at adulthood.

PRICKLY DOGFISH—*OXYNOTUS BRUNIENSIS*

Not enough is known about this strangely shaped shark, one of five species of small sharks with rough skin and pronounced ridges on their sides. They have two dorsal fins, and the tip of the first one looks crumpled, a bit like the sorting hat in the Harry Potter films.

They live in what is called the Twilight Zone of the ocean. Scientists call it the mesopelagic zone, and it's the layer below the one that sunlight penetrates—about 660–3,300 feet down. Some light still gets there, just not a lot. Most commonly,

the prickly dogfish hangs out from 990 to 2,150 feet.

They eat creatures that live on the bottom, such as worms, crustaceans, and mollusks, and they live off the coasts of New Zealand and southern Australia. Not a lot is known about their reproductive habits, but they're believed to produce litters of seven or more pups, which hatch inside the mother before they swim out.

Not enough is known about them to determine whether they're endangered, threatened, or reproducing adequately.

INDONESIAN CARPETSHARK—*HEMISCYLLIUM FREYCINETI*

Why are these called carpetsharks? Two reasons: they spend their lives lying on the seafloor, and they're extravagantly patterned, like the world's most beautiful rugs. Carpetsharks come in many varieties, with 39 species known. The Indonesian species, which is spotted like a leopard, lives in shallow, sandy waters and on coral reefs.

Not all that much is known about these sharks, although they lay their eggs externally and don't get longer than two feet or so. What's particularly fascinating about these wildly patterned creatures is that they don't really swim. They wiggle along the bottom, pushing themselves with their pectoral and pelvic fins.

Experts would love to know more about this shark, to make sure its survival isn't threatened by the practice of blast fishing that occurs in the area. This is when fishermen set off dynamite underwater, stunning fish for easy capture.

VIPER DOGFISH—*TRIGONOGNATHUS KABEYAI*

There's not really a tactful way to say this, but if you were going to cast a hideous villain for your underwater movie, the viper dogfish definitely looks the part. It's black on the bottom and dark brown on top, and it has a face like a snake's, with huge, curving, pointed teeth set into a grinning jaw that can be extended to wolf down prey.

They kill by protruding their jaws and impaling fish and crustaceans on their oversize teeth. And they swallow their food whole. To top things off, they are believed to glow in the dark.

These are very rare sharks, the last in their genus. They live in the north and central Pacific, near Japan and the Hawaiian Islands, preferring to

prowl the upper continental slopes—a ledge of land that tilts downward from a flat continental shelf and leads toward the deep ocean floor, roughly 1,100–1,200 feet below sea level.

Not enough is known about the viper dogfish to be certain how they reproduce. They're tiny, despite their fierce appearance, topping out at around 14 to 17 inches. So they could maybe only be the villains in a miniseries.

PACIFIC ANGELSHARK—*SQUATINA CALIFORNICA*

You might think this shark is a ray or a skate. It's flat. It has wide pectoral fins that flare out from its body like wings. It also has a tail fin with a bigger lobe on the bottom—the opposite of the way shark's caudal fins usually appear. But it's a shark. The giveaways: its pectoral fins aren't fully attached, its gill slits curve around its head, and its mouth is in front of its head, not under.

All angelsharks have gray bellies. Some have patterned backs for camouflage in the mud and sand—the *californica* has dark brown or blackish blotches. They have big mouths and nostrils, and white edges around their pectoral and pelvic fins. One fascinating thing about angelsharks: we know there are more species of them than have been

identified and described by scientists.

This angelshark lives in coastal waters in the northeast Pacific Ocean, on continental shelves as deep as 650 feet. They don't swim long distances, preferring to ambush prey at night. They get about five feet long and can live 35 years.

Their gestation period is about the same as the human one: nine to ten months. Six to ten pups are in a litter, and they're about 10 inches long when they're born live (these are viviparous sharks). They are a near-threatened species because fishermen caught them until their numbers dropped to dangerously low levels in the 1990s. Great white sharks also eat them.

DAGGERNOSE SHARK—*ISOGOMPHODON OXYRHYNCHUS*

These small sharks live in the tropical west Atlantic waters off the northern coast of South America, in cloudy waters found in estuaries, mangroves, and river mouths. They don't get much longer than four and a half feet, and have long, pointed noses, large paddle-shaped pectoral fins, tiny eyes, and facial expressions that look a bit surprised. (The snouts and eyes are probably an adaptation for life in the murky waters they prefer.)

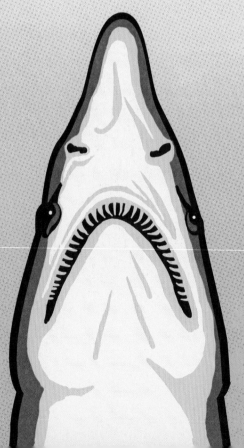

These diminutive predators aren't a threat to people, but they have become a critically endangered species because they get caught in the nets of fishermen. It's a big problem for these sharks because they reproduce slowly. Females aren't ready to reproduce until they're six or seven years old. Males need to be five or six. Gestation takes another year for the sharks to produce a litter of pups. They have between two and eight at a time, and they reproduce viviparously.

ZEBRA SHARK—*STEGOSTOMA FASCIATUM*

Zebra sharks are beautiful to behold. Their tail fins are broad and as long as their bodies. They have small mouths that look a bit like letter slots, and they have little barbels hanging down over them. They're strong swimmers and able to work their flexible bodies into crevices as they pursue bony fish (and maybe sea snakes). They also eat crustaceans and mollusks.

But the most remarkable part about them: when zebra sharks are born, they have stripes. As they age, those stripes turn into spots. Sometimes people mistakenly call them leopard sharks, but they're not.

Zebra sharks live on coral reefs near the shores of the western Pacific Ocean from Japan to Australia, as well as the Indian Ocean and the Red Sea. They can grow up to 12 feet long, although most are in the seven-and-a-half-foot range.

Not many predators threaten zebra sharks. Sometimes larger sharks will eat them, but their chief adversary is humans, who eat their meat fresh or preserved in salt, and also turn it into fishmeal, which is used as fertilizer or in animal foods.

GREENLAND SHARK—*SOMNIOSUS MICROCEPHALUS*

This is the slowest shark in the ocean. It's so slow it's called a sleeper shark. The *microcephalus* part of its name refers to its tiny head. But that's the only tiny thing about this creature, which lives in the north Atlantic and Arctic and is one of the most unusual sharks we know. They're 8–14 feet long on average, but can top 21 feet. They take a long time to get this big, though, because the water they inhabit is so very cold.

They eat lots of different things: smaller sharks, skates, eels, herring, and other fish. And even though they're poky, they've been known to eat seals, probably when the seals are sleeping underwater to avoid being eaten by polar bears. Some Greenland shark stomachs have been cut open to reveal the remains of horses. One had eaten a polar bear. And one an entire reindeer, antlers and all. They're attracted to stinky meat and often eat dead animals in the water, or gather around fisheries.

Nothing eats the Greenland shark, though—at least not the whole thing. It's too big. But it does commonly get a parasite called a copepod. These little creatures, a type of crustacean, find their way onto the tiny eyes of the Greenland shark and make themselves at home there. This can make the shark blind, but the shark can function without eyesight.

Meanwhile, the meat of the Greenland shark is poisonous and smells like pee. People do eat it, though. It has to be carefully prepared. If it's not, it causes symptoms that make the eater seem drunk. (Sometimes dogs will eat the meat and stagger around.) The meat can be boiled, dried, fermented underground, or rinsed repeatedly in clean water. It is said to taste so bad that it makes people throw up until they're used to the flavor.

Captured for their liver oil, this is a near-threatened species.

PYJAMA SHARK—*PORODERMA AFRICANUM*

Also know as the striped catshark, this striking nocturnal species lives off the coast of South Africa in the southeast Atlantic Ocean and western Indian Ocean. It likes rocky reefs inshore and offshore, and can be found as deep as 328 feet below the surface, where it hangs out in caves and cracks during the day before coming out at night to hunt crustaceans, cephalopods, mollusks, worms, and bony fish. They also eat smaller sharks and shark eggs, and larger sharks eat them.

Pyjama sharks are dark gray with black stripes running from their noses to their tails. The *poroderma* part of their name means "skin with pores," and it describes the hard dermal denticles that cover their bodies. They can reach sizes of about 40 inches for the males, and about 36 for the females, though the average is smaller.

They reproduce by laying brown egg cases shaped like little purses, with streaming handles that attach to plants and other objects. The hatchlings are just under six inches long at birth.

SHARPNOSE SEVENGILL SHARK—*HEPTRANCHIAS PERLO*

If you want to find a living fossil shark, meaning one that's really similar to the sort swimming during the Jurassic era, the sharpnose sevengill is a great candidate. Their skeletons and digestive systems are simpler than those of species that evolved later. They also don't have nictitating membranes on their eyes, which are big and fluorescent green.

These sharks don't exceed about four and a half feet, and are usually quite a bit smaller. Their bodies are long and slender, and a gray-brown color on top, though their bellies are pale.

They're harmless, unless you eat them or try to capture them. Their skin is mildly toxic to humans, and they are aggressive biters. Despite their small size, they're fierce predators, especially at night, and eat shrimp, crabs, lobsters, squid, cuttlefish, smaller sharks, and rays. Larger sharks feed on them.

You can find sharpnose sevengills in tropical and temperate oceans around the world, except the northeast Pacific. Because they are so widespread, they are believed to be excellent swimmers. They do like the deep water, spending most of their time anywhere from 89–3,280 feet below.

They are aplacental viviparous, which means their eggs hatch inside the mother, who gives birth to 6–20 pups per litter.

BIRDBEAK DOGFISH—*DEANIA CALCEA*

This strange-looking shark is well named. Also called a shovelnose spiny dogfish or brier shark, it has a pointy, flat snout that really does make it look birdlike.

These grow up to three feet long. They're gray to dark brown in color, darker on the fins and above their eyes and gills. They live in the east Atlantic Ocean from Iceland to South Africa, and in the Pacific near Japan, Taiwan, Australia, New Zealand, Peru, and Chile. They occupy deepwater continental shelves and slopes, from about 230 feet to about 4,750 feet below the surface. They're aplacental viviparous and bear litters of about six to twelve, researchers believe (based on pregnant specimens they've found).

Their diet includes hatchetfish, shrimp, and an equally strange-looking fish called the scaly dragonfish, which itself is a weird creature—it has a huge mouth, curving teeth, and a glowing barbel that hangs from its chin like a beard and is used to lure prey.

HORN SHARK—*HETERODONTUS FRANCISCI*

Some sharks migrate long distances. Not the horn shark. The farthest this animal has been observed to travel is 10 miles. In warmer months, they tend to swim about 7–36 feet below the surface, though they've been found in caves as deep as 656 feet. They migrate into deeper water during winter, when they hang out below 98 feet deep. They like warm waters and can be found in the kelp forests of the eastern Pacific Ocean from central California to the Gulf of California.

They're strange looking, with piglike snouts, and they get their name from the prickly spike in front of each of their dorsal fins. It's possible these spikes are protective. There's video footage of a baby horn shark that gets swallowed—and promptly spit

out—by an angelshark. (The baby swam off, as if the whole thing was no big deal.)

Horn sharks have impressive teeth. They're not fangs like a great white's, though. They have two kinds: small hooked teeth in front, meant for grabbing prey, and molarlike side teeth they use for grinding. The horn sharks that like to eat sea urchins sometimes have purple stains on their teeth and dorsal spines.

They hunt at night, and researchers suspect their ampullae of Lorenzini are important because these sharks have been known to bite electrodes that generate the same electromagnetic frequency as that generated by their prey. They're creatures of habit, prowling an area of the rocky seafloor the size of an Olympic swimming pool with slow movements of their pelvic and pectoral fins. During the day they rest (and the ones who hide their heads tend to wear their skin away).

Horn shark egg cases are particularly spectacular. About a week or two after mating, the female horn shark lays two egg cases every 11 to 14 days for four months. They're a glossy caramel color and they spiral like drill bits. They often tuck them under rocks to keep safe, and as the shark pups gestate, the cases turn dark brown. Sometimes big snails poke through the cases and suck out the yolks, killing the pup inside. Northern elephant seals also sometimes eat the egg cases and the juvenile sharks. And believe it or not, bald eagles sometimes pluck small horn sharks from shallow water and eat them.

WHALE SHARKS—*RHINCODON TYPUS*

The next time you look at a school bus, squint for a minute and pretend you're looking at a whale shark. These magnificent beasts can get as long as a school bus, and they can weigh more than 40,000 pounds. This makes them the world's biggest fish (at least the biggest one alive today). Their mouths alone can get up to almost five feet wide.

Whale sharks are filter feeders. They swim near the surface with their huge mouths open wide, sucking up small fish, shrimp, krill, and plankton, which is made of microscopic plants and animals floating through the sea. Whale sharks sniff out plankton- and protein-rich water. Then they slurp in a gulp, close their mouths, and expel the water through their big gills. What remains are solid food particles under two centimeters across. And if anything sticks in their gills, they cough it out later.

Whale sharks are docile. Sometimes swimmers have even hitched rides on their fins. Whale sharks do have very rough and thick skin, though, so it's not something that should be done without great care.

SWELL SHARKS— *CEPHALOSCYLLIUM VENTRIOSUM*

The swell shark isn't particularly remarkable looking. It doesn't have frills or spikes. It has a short snout, a wide body, and big oval eyes. It's also not a large creature. At most, they get to about 43 inches long. But if you blew one up to the size of a great white, the swell shark would have the bigger mouth of the two.

It puts its big mouth to interesting use. If a predator comes after it as it's lurking in a crevice, the swell shark bends itself in half and takes hold of its tail with its mouth. It gulps in water or air, depending on whether it's below

water or at the surface. In doing so, it balloons to twice its size. This makes it harder to bite, and harder to yank from its hiding spot. After the danger has passed, the shark barks and expels the water or air, returning to normal size.

These nocturnal hunters feed on mollusks and crustaceans and live in the eastern Pacific Ocean from central California to the Gulf of Mexico and in central Chile. They lay pale eggs that attach to rocks with rubbery tentacles. These darken as the pups gestate and hatch within 9–12 months, depending on the water temperature.

GHOST SHARKS—*CALLORHINCHUS MILII*

Though they're called ghost sharks, these creatures aren't really sharks at all. They're chimaeras, which are related to sharks, rays, and skates (and whorl sharks, which are extinct). These silvery creatures live deep in the southwest Pacific, along the coasts of New Zealand and Australia. They have elephant-like snouts (and are sometimes even called elephant fish or elephant sharks), a single gill on each side, and huge pectoral fins that they flap like wings to propel them slowly underwater. They use their floppy snouts to detect food and sift it from the sand. Their eyes are enormous, their skin is smooth, and their dorsal fin has a spine—with venom in it.

They're not huge, topping out at around 49

inches, and they live for an estimated 15 years. They reproduce by laying eggs, and these egg cases look weird, like a cockroach that's been run over by a truck. They lay their eggs two at a time, and the cases are about 10 inches long. Over an eight-month gestation period, they turn from golden to black.

But they are interesting for more than their strange looks. They're living fossils, the oldest living group of vertebrates with jaws, nearly unchanged for 400 million years. It's because they live so deep in the ocean—more than 650 feet below—an environment that is so remote and stable that their evolution has been negligible. This is a source of fascination and insight for scientists, who have sequenced the creature's genome and are using the information to understand how bones might have evolved.

Other sharks eat the ghost shark. So do humans—its flesh is often turned into the fish part of fish and chips (and it's called a silver trumpeter or whitefish fillet). Their population is stable, though, and they are not on any watch lists.

PREHISTORIC SHARKS

Sharks have been around for more than 400 million years. Some species, like the ghost shark, are similar to sharks that lived long ago. But some spectacular sharks we can only learn through the fossil record.

WHORL SHARK

This 270-million-year-old creature has been a mystery for more than a century. In 1899, a Russian geologist found a fossil in Kazakhstan. He named the nearly 20-foot fish *Helicoprion*, a word that means "spiral saw." It was an apt name—somewhere on this creature's body, a spiral of teeth grew. The geologist, Alexander Petrovich, wasn't sure where the spiral fit because the curve of fangs had been detached from the shark's body.

For years, researchers made their best guesses. It seemed an unwieldy thing for a creature to carry in its mouth—did it attach to the back like a weapon? Was it part of the tail? Most supposed this fearsome whorl of fangs was used for defense.

That changed as more fossils were discovered. In 1950, a Danish paleontologist found an important new specimen in an Idaho mine. It had cranial cartilage in it, which meant the whorl was at least partially in the mouth.

For decades, researchers made their best

guesses about how this spiral of teeth might have fit in or around the shark's mouth. Then new technology offered a better view. A high-resolution X-ray scanner in Texas was used to create a 3-D computer model of the shark's skull.

They learned that the whorl of teeth sat all the way inside the shark's mouth, like a tongue. Rather than being used as a defense weapon, the tooth spiral helped the shark slice its prey into small pieces. Whorl sharks had no top teeth, so when they closed their jaws, the spiral of teeth pushed back, cut the fish and cephalopods, and sent the chunks down the hatch.

In all, the whorl shark's jaw could have contained more than 150 teeth, and could have been nearly 20 inches long. That said, further study has shown that the whorl shark probably isn't a shark at all. It does have sharklike teeth, but it's closer to a ratfish, which is a chimaera.

This is one of the problems with common names—they can be misleading. This is why scientists use the formal two-word naming system that describes the species and identifies its genus.

MEGALODON

Imagine a shark three times as long as a great white. Longer than a school bus. As tall as a brachiosaurus—more than 50 feet (and maybe as long as 59 feet). This is the megalodon, a name that means "big tooth," and it's apt. Some of the teeth were about seven inches long.

The megalodon has been extinct for 2.6 million years. It's the largest shark that's been discovered and one of the largest predators in the history of the world. What we know of it, we've pieced together from the evidence that remains: fossilized vertebrae and teeth, some of which are wider than an adult's hand.

Those remains are enough to make a solid guess about how big these animals truly were, though.

When humans first found megalodon teeth, we weren't sure what they were. Centuries ago, people thought they were the petrified tongues of dragons. Or perhaps moon rocks. But then a seventeenth-century naturalist named Nicholas Steno recognized them as shark teeth. Very, very large shark teeth that had been fossilized. Unlike the largest sharks alive today, the megalodon didn't eat krill and plankton. It ate *whales*.

In addition to the teeth, the vertebrae that have been found have been important tools for building a picture of the megalodon. Called centra, these have rings that tell the shark's age and how fast it grew.

What's more, fossilized bones of other animals show that the megalodon was an even fiercer hunter than the great white, which attacks from below and waits for its prey to bleed to death. The megalodon didn't bother. There are whale rib fossils with megalodon tooth marks in them. These fossils sometimes tell amazing stories. There's one whale rib bone with three puncture wounds from a megalodon—and it looks as though the whale survived for a few weeks, because the bone shows evidence of responding to an infection.

Even though they didn't always get their prey, the megalodon had an incredibly strong bite, the strongest of any animal recorded. With living animals, this is measured by putting a device between a pair of teeth and measuring the pressure. Crocodiles, one of the most powerful biters, have been shown to exert 3,700 pounds of pressure per square inch with their jaws. Megalodons are thought to have had a 24,400-to-41,000-pound chomp.

Their relatives today include great whites and makos.

MORE PREHISTORIC SHARK BITES

The first-known shark placoid scales come from a shark called Elegestolepis. That's the only evidence we have for this animal, which dates back 420 million years to the Silurian period. It might not be the oldest shark, but it's certainly ancient.

The Golden Age of Sharks was during the Carboniferous period, from 360 to 286 million years ago. There were at least 45 different shark families. The male Stethacanthus had a dorsal fin that looked like an anvil. It also had a flat spiky surface on top of its head, and no one's quite sure why.

Another shark alive during this time, Edestus, had strange teeth. The name means "devour," and their single row of jagged fangs pushed forward, like pinking shears, a type of scissors that cuts zigzags.

A Cretaceous-period shark named Cretoxyrhina had an extra-thick layer of enamel on its teeth, making them harder than usual. It's been nicknamed the "Ginsu" shark after the freakishly sharp knives sold on television, and experts think the teeth were hard enough to bite through bones and shells. To make things scarier, this shark was more than 22 feet long—bigger than a great white.

WEIRDEST S

There are weird sharks, and there are sharks with weird names. Here are some of the most entertaining:

BLIND SHARK

This small shark lives off the eastern coast of Australia. It's named for the way it sucks in its eyeballs and closes its eyelids when it's taken out of the water.

BUMPY-TAIL RAGGED-TOOTH SHARK

Also known as smalltooth sand tigers, these rare sharks look like they're scowling. They live in deep water in warm and tropical seas around the world.

COOKIECUTTER SHARK

Also known as cigar sharks for their long shape, these parasitic fish are known for using their sharp teeth to cut a cookie-shaped wheel of meat out of the sides of their victims.

CLOWN CATSHARK

These live in the Indian Ocean and Andaman Sea and get their name because the spots below their pointy dorsal fins look like clown faces.

COBBLER WOBBEGONG

There are many kinds of wobbe-gongs, but this is the only one to have big bumps on its head and body for its whole life. Not that the shark cares, but it's probably fortunate it's not called the warty wobbegong.

CRYING IZAK AND GRINNING IZAK

Izak is a variation of the name Isaac, which means "laughter." The crying Izak seems to have black tear marks in front of its eyes. The grinning Izak doesn't, and it has a wider, smilier mouth.

CYRANO SPURDOG SHARK

Cyrano de Bergerac was a French novelist and playwright from the 1600s. A play written about him made fun of his nose. The cyrano spurdog has a really long, really broad snout, which means that for more than 300 years, people have been making fun of the Frenchman's nose.

DARK SHYSHARK

When these sharks get scared, they curl up and cover their eyes. These sharks live off the coast of southern Namibia and western South Africa.

FAT CATSHARK

Catsharks get their names because their eyes are almond-shaped, like cat's eyes. Not a lot is known about these sharks, which live only in the deep waters of the East China Sea.

HARK NAMES

GOLLUMSHARK

These sharks are also known as slender smoothhounds because they're skinny, but their better name refers to the character in J. R. R. Tolkien's books. Their full species name is *Gollum suluensis*, named for the Sulu Sea, not for the Star Trek character. (The character is actually named after the sea.)

GREY GUMMY SHARK

These sharks get their name from their teeth, which are flat and pave the tops of their gums. They're used to crush prey, and they live in the waters of southern Australia.

THE "HAPPY" SHARKS

There are several kinds of shark named happy—the Happy Eddie, Happy Chappie, Plain Happy, and Pretty Happy. The "happy" comes from their genus name, *haploblepharus*, which means "single eyelid."

LOLLIPOP CATSHARK

These sharks get their name because they have giant, round heads attached to slender bodies. They live in the eastern Pacific, between southern Baja California and the Gulf of California, Mexico.

NERVOUS SHARK

This type of requiem shark gets its name because people make it nervous. It's common and found in the shallow, warm, coastal waters of northern Australia, Papua New Guinea, and the Solomon Islands.

PIGEYE SHARK

Also knows as a Java shark, this creature has a short and blunt snout and small, piggy eyes. They live in the warm, coastal waters of the eastern Atlantic and western Indo-Pacific oceans.

WHISKERY SHARK

These natives of southern and western Australia are medium size and thin, with prominent barbels that hang from their snouts like hipster mustaches.

MIND-BLOWING SHARK FACTS

SHARKS LOVE HEAVY METAL

Death metal is a form of loud and fast rock music whose lyrics focus on death, mayhem, destruction, and other dark things. A Discovery crew trying to lure a great white named Joan of Shark lowered speakers into the water and blasted some death metal. Joan didn't arrive, but two other great whites did. They suspect the low-frequency vibrations of the music sounded like the death throes of fish.

Rock on, great whites. Rock on.

SHARKS THAT LIVE IN A VOLCANO

There's an active underwater volcano off the Solomon Islands. Called Kavachi, it erupts at irregular intervals, and you can see and hear it from 10 miles away. Needless to say, it's not someplace you'd want to be when it's blasting hot lava, ash, and steam.

A group of researchers lowered a robot and underwater cameras into the water, hoping to learn as much as they could about the volcano's geology and chemistry.

Much to their surprise, they filmed hammerhead and silky sharks living in the volcano, where the water is hot and so acidic it has burned divers, and where carbon dioxide and methane gas bubbles up from vents in the seafloor, even when the volcano isn't actively erupting.

It's a hellish environment, but somehow, the sharks survive it.

SOME SHARKS CAN'T MOVE IF YOU FLIP THEM OVER

Some animals—sharks among them—freeze when you flip them over. Their muscles relax, and their breathing becomes slow and rhythmic. This state, called tonic immobility, takes less than a minute to set in, and it works on a variety of sharks, including spiny dogfish, lemon sharks, leopard sharks, and blacktip and whitetip reef sharks. Fishermen and researchers immobilize sharks to reduce their chances of getting injured when they're forced to handle them.

Experts believe that flipping a shark over changes the way its sensory organs work. Not all sharks reach tonic immobility by being turned upside down, though. Tiger sharks go boneless when you cover the skin around their eyes, where their ampullae of Lorenzini are.

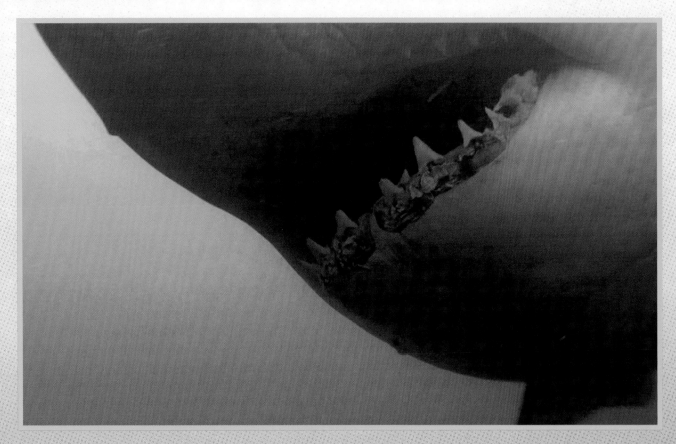

FOUR OUT OF FIVE DENTISTS WOULD LIKE YOU TO HAVE SHARK TEETH

Fluoride helps protect the enamel of teeth, which is why many types of toothpaste contain it, why some cities put it into the tap water, and why dentists sometimes make you hold trays of weird-tasting goo in your mouth. Tooth enamel is made of fluorapatite, which resists the acid that bacteria in your mouth produce, causing cavities. Shark teeth are covered in fluoride. So, not only do sharks grow new teeth all of the time, they're unlikely to get cavities.

NO ONE KNOWS WHERE THE NAME *SHARK* CAME FROM

The best guess seems to be that the word entered the English language in London in 1569, when a British pirate and slave smuggler named Captain John Hawkins returned with a shark that he put on display. It's possible that this word comes from the Mayan word *xoc*, which might have meant shark.

(Hawkins stopped being a slaver and became treasurer of the British Navy in 1577. He later became an English knight after defending England against the invading Spanish armada.)

MEN GET MORE SHARK BITES THAN WOMEN DO

Statistically, more than 90 percent of the human victims of shark bites have been men. But experts don't think this is because sharks prefer the taste or smell. Rather, it's that men have been more likely historically to be swimming long distances, diving, surfing, and waging warfare.

A FEMALE WHALE SHARK CAN BE PREGNANT WITH MORE THAN ONE LITTER AT A TIME

Some sharks give birth to shark pups that have different fathers. What this means was that they mated with more than one shark around the same time, and different males fertilized different eggs.

Whale sharks appear to be capable of doing something different, and something really unusual in nature. They can be pregnant with several different litters at the same time—and the pups all have the same father.

A University of Chicago–Illinois research team

studied a pregnant whale shark caught in 1995 off the coast of Taiwan. Inside, they found 304 embryos. Some of them were still encased in eggs. Others were nearly ready to be born. They studied the DNA of the pups and determined that all of them had the same father.

It's strange for nature, and strange for sharks, and it seems the female whale shark is able to store sperm and use it to fertilize eggs later. The reasons for this might stay a mystery for a good long time, because it's illegal to capture whale sharks and they're not often found in aquariums.

HEADS OR TAILS?

Some sharks hatch from eggs. Of the ones that are born live, baby sharks are usually born tail first. But sand sharks and hammerheads are born head first.

THE CURIOUS CASE OF THE MOSES SOLE

Sharks have extremely sensitive senses, and some scientists think you could drive sharks off by overwhelming them. (Think about how you'd flee a room with a horrible smell or extremely loud noise.)

And while there could be very good reason to develop shark repellents like this to keep sharks away from people, it's probably even better for the sharks than the people who fear them. Humans kill vastly more sharks than sharks do humans. About 12 million sharks are inadvertently snagged each year by fishermen, who hate catching them because their rough skin is really hard on the fish they're trying to haul in.

The history of research into shark repellents, though, has been a military task. Shark attacks were a big problem in World War II, and scientists tried to develop repellents that smelled like dead shark, thinking that would keep them way.

Julia Child, who later became a world-famous chef, but worked as a spy during the war, tried unsuccessfully to make something that could be used on explosives targeting submarines, but it inadvertently kept attracting sharks.

It wasn't until the 1970s that researchers started looking into a chemical given off by the Moses sole, a fish that looks like a flounder and lives in the Red Sea. You can kill a shark by injecting the chemical into its mouth. Researchers tried using this scent on US Navy spy devices being dragged behind submarines in the 1980s because sharks were biting them and ruining entire missions. Again, the attempt to create an effective repellent was a bust.

In the early 2000s, researchers returned to the World War II idea of making something smell like dead shark. Using better tools for analyzing the chemicals, they came up with one that smells like feet. Apparently this makes sharks stop eating, even when they're in a frenzy. Another approach is using magnets to overwhelm a shark's electromagnetic sense receptors. So far, nothing has been completely effective, but the researchers say their goal is to reduce sharks killed inadvertently (as well as bites to humans).

A WHALE OF AN EGG

A whale shark egg measured 12 inches long, 5.5 inches wide, and was 3.5 inches thick. It's the largest egg of any living animal recorded.

SHARK WASH!

Sometimes scalloped hammerhead sharks become infected with parasites such as leeches and copepods on their skin and in their mouths. When this happens, they visit cleaning stations manned by cleaner wrasses, active little striped fish that eat the parasites in exchange for protection from the sharks.

The process is fascinating. When a parasite-ridden shark swims up, the cleaner wrasses move up and down, as if in greeting. The "client," as the shark is called, recognizes the cleaner wrasse by its stripes (sort of the way you might recognize a car wash attendant by his or her uniform). When the sharks have recognized the cleaner, they get into a position to be cleaned, by opening their mouths or gills.

WEIRDEST MEALS EVER

Sometimes sharks eat weird things. But before we get all judgmental, consider the fact that dogs sometimes eat weird things. There is X-ray evidence proving that dogs have eaten knives, rubber ducks, and electric blankets. And it's not just dogs. A snake once swallowed a pair of lightbulbs. Humans, meanwhile, have been known to swallow swords, jewelry, and coins. There's even a disorder called pica that makes people want to eat clay, drywall, chalk, glass, sand, and other nonfood items.

Suffice it to say sharks aren't alone when it comes to eating unexpected things. Shark stomachs have been found to contain boots, license plates, rope, clothing, wire, baseballs, old tires, an unopened can of salmon and—get this—a suit of armor. The tiger shark is especially known for eating a lot of weird stuff. It's a good thing sharks can barf their stomachs out and suck them back in when they need to.

But what about weird stuff that is actually food? Here are some unusual meals known to have been eaten by sharks:

A POLAR BEAR.
Scientists studying shark-hunting habits in the Norwegian Arctic archipelago of Svalbard found part of the jaw of a juvenile polar bear in a shark's belly. Did the shark catch and eat the bear? It's impossible to say—and it might have just munched on a carcass. Even so, whoa.

A REINDEER.
Greenland has 27,000 miles of coast-line, and there has been only a single recorded shark attack along all of it, which makes it one of the least dangerous seashores in the world, at least for peo-ple. This isn't the case for reindeer and caribou—two land animals that have been found in the stomach of this rare shark.

A PORCUPINE.
A tiger shark in Australia was found with porcupine spines in its stomach. Ouch.

TWO WHALES.
You might have heard of turducken, which is a chicken stuffed into a duck stuffed into a turkey. There exists a 35-million-year-old-fossil sharwhalin—a whale that ate a whale and then was eaten by a shark. (It's also possible the medium-size whale was pregnant.)

This strange and wonderful fossil was found in Egypt's Valley of the Whales. All of the animals in question were enormous. The whale was a Basilo-saurus, which could grow up to 65 feet long. The shark was even bigger.

A 200-POUND SEA LION.
Mako sharks usually eat herring and tuna. And yet a 12-foot-long mako shark was found with a 200-pound sea lion in its stomach. Small for a sea lion, but a very big meal for this shark.

A WOODPECKER.
How does a land bird get inside the belly of a shark? They might be drawn by the lights of something like an oilrig. These trips tend to be one-way. Scientists have found birds—including a woodpecker—in the bellies of sharks.

AN INTACT HORSE'S HEAD.
An 11-foot tiger shark in Australia was found with one of these in its gut.

CHAPTER FOUR

SHARK FIGHT!
SHARKS VERSUS OTHER PREDATORS

We know sharks are incredible predators. But in a battle between sharks and other epic fighters, who would win? It's a question we can't resist. The blood. The fangs. The fur. The cartilage . . . the thought makes us giddy.

Using a combination of data, fighting style, and imagination, we're going to delve into this very matter, without anything pesky like geography, habitat, or time period getting in the way.

MEGALODON ⭐VS SPINOSAURUS

The Cretaceous period was the time of giant dinosaurs. Spinosaurus was one of the biggest, outweighing the average Tyrannosaurus rex by a whopping two tons.

A Spinosaurus could be an estimated 50 feet long, 20 feet tall, and weigh somewhere between six and nine *tons*. What's more, paleontologists recently decided that Spinosaurus spent most of its time in the water. Their clue? The dinosaur has short (but strong) hind legs, flat feet, and dense skeletal structure. Think giant penguin with fangs.

Whether on land or at sea, Spinosaurus would be fearsome. They're named for the large spines on their backs, which were seven feet long and webbed with skin, so they looked like sails. Can you imagine swimming and seeing that sail knife through the water like a giant shark fin? Yikes. Their long, slender snouts and needlelike teeth made them great at catching their prey—mostly fish. But from time to time, they ate sharks.

We've paired this formidable ancient beast with another gigantic blast-from-the-past, the megalodon. The name *mega-lodon* means "giant tooth," and that was no lie. Some of the bigger teeth that have been found were seven inches long. To give you some idea of how huge these teeth are, great white teeth top out at three inches. Not only were megalodon teeth big, but there were a lot of them—about 276, arranged in five rows along the jaw. Serrated and thick, their teeth evolved to tear through flippers, spine and bone.

And it's not just their teeth: Everything about this shark was huge. They measured between 50–60 feet long and weighed between 50–100 tons. On land, this size would make them unwieldy. In the water, they would have been fast and nimble hunters, swimming at an estimated 20 miles an hour.

WHO WOULD WIN IN A FIGHT?

Although the Spinosaurus literally ate sharks for breakfast, Megalodon would dominate in a fang-to-fang fight. Despite its gigantic size, the elongated shape of the Spinosaurus skull meant the animal had a relatively weak bite, paleontologists speculate. Their narrow snouts and pointy teeth would make them deadly in close combat, but most likely the fight would be over before they got their shot.

The Megalodon also greatly outweighed the Spinosaurus. This gigantic shark would most likely have ambushed the dinosaur, tearing off that giant spine and those clawed hands with its strong, serrated teeth that were evolved to tear cartilage and crush bone. Once the dinosaur was rendered immobile, the Megalodon would make quick work of its meal.

LION VS TIGER SHARK

Lions, the mighty royalty of the grasslands . . . muscular . . . majestic in looks . . . committed to naps (up to 20 hours a day). But don't let their yawning fool you. They're fierce predators. Between their size and their mighty roar, lions have a high intimidation factor—even when facing off the garbage mouth of the sea, the tiger shark.

Lions are patient and organized hunters. They use many different tactics, depending on their prey. They hunt in packs, each lion taking on different

assigned places, with most of the hunting handled by the smaller, lighter females. Or they'll lie in wait, perfectly camouflaged, around a waterhole. They might also stalk their prey, sprinting in short, last-minute bursts up to 50 miles per hour.

Of the large cats, lions actually have a fairly weak bite for their size, measuring in at around 650 pounds per square inch. But that doesn't mean their bite isn't lethal. What's more, their massive, claw-tipped paws pack a wallop.

Tiger sharks range from 10–14 feet in length, and often weigh between 800–1,400 pounds. They're aggressive, solitary hunters, and will even attack other tiger sharks. They, too, rely on their camouflage to hide them from prey and predator.

Tiger sharks are scavengers that will eat almost anything, including other sharks, stingrays, seals, birds, tires, and even license plates. They are fast, topping out at 20 miles per hour, though they can manage short bursts of higher speed if they need to. Between their excellent senses, quick turning ability, and wicked serrated teeth, tiger sharks are fearsome predators.

WHO WOULD WIN IN A FIGHT?

Imagine you are watching a lion safely through a pair of binoculars. The giant tawny cat dips her head for a drink, only to be surprised by a swift and brutal attack from a tiger shark. For whatever reason, lions don't pay attention to which way the wind is blowing, meaning they don't notice if they are approaching something from downwind or upwind. With the tiger shark's excellent senses, this would be a huge mistake.

However, let's imagine for a moment the lion isn't alone. Maybe it seems like cheating, pitting one tiger shark against a pride of lions. Odds are, that's what the fight would be like because lions are cooperative hunters. The tiger shark is big, fast, and deadly, and might get in a few good chomps, but he simply wouldn't make it against an entire pride.

KODIAK BEAR ⭐VS⭐ GREAT WHITE

Kodiak bears are the biggest subspecies of brown bear alive. When they're on all fours, they measure in around five feet tall. Standing, they can get up to 10 feet high. If a Kodiak bear came into your house, he'd have to duck or his head would go through the ceiling. They're also heavy. Males tip the scales anywhere from 800–1,500 pounds. The sows usually weigh between 500–700 pounds, but you still wouldn't want to get between one and her cubs.

They have four-inch, nonretractable claws for digging, foraging, and hunting, and they can reach speeds of 35–40 miles an hour for short distances. This is faster than the fastest human, Usain Bolt, who averaged 23.35 miles per hour in his world-record-setting 100-meter dash.

Kodiak heads are bigger and broader than the average brown bear. Their coats are longer and shaggier, and they're so strong they can crush a bowling ball in their jaws. Not that they'd eat one. Even omnivores like Kodiaks have their limits. The large, distinctive hump on their back is solid muscle.

Though they're generally solitary creatures, they will share territory if needed and have developed a language involving attitude, vocalization and posturing.

Great whites also tend to be solitary, but sometimes gather to hunt in groups. The average great white shark can be between 15–20 feet long, and can weigh up to 5,000 pounds. Female great whites are far larger than the males. To give you some perspective, if you had three adults lie down head to toe, that's about how big a great white is.

Their senses of smell, sight, hearing, and taste, and even electromagnetic energy are extraordinary. They can swim 15 miles an hour, and usually ambush their prey from below, digging into the soft underbelly of a seal or sea lion with their fangs. Great white sharks have more than 300 triangular, serrated teeth, perfect for tearing things apart. They pin their prey with the bottom teeth, and clamp down with the top, flicking their tails to shake their prey from side to side to tear away a hunk of meat.

Sharks use camouflage and their environment to great effect. A seal looking down would be unlikely to see the great white, because its gray back blends in with the seafloor. The light filtering through the water would also make it harder to see the pale-bellied shark from below. The shark, on the other hand, has an excellent view of the seal from below (even though they sometimes mistake humans in wetsuits and on surfboards as seals).

WHO WOULD WIN IN A FIGHT?

Great whites attack vertically. Their torpedo-shaped bodies are perfectly tapered to shoot through the water, and even above the surface in a dramatic breach. This attack angle also makes it difficult to spot the shark because it makes it look smaller. If a great white were able to use this style and managed to ambush a Kodiak, it could easily be game over.

But it's not over just yet for our fierce friend, the Kodiak. While the great white has a tremendous bite and is amazingly fast, it would be hard to get a grip on the Kodiak because of its thick coat. If the bear survived the initial attack, it could regain the advantage.

The Kodiak is strong and has long claws, which could easily lay waste to the eyes and sensitive gills of the shark. While the shark's skin is tough, it's nowhere near as hard as a bowling ball, which the Kodiak is equipped to destroy.

Like the shark, Kodiaks are fast, smart, adaptive hunters. The sharks are big and heavy, too, but a brown bear can play catch with a Dumpster. They are so well matched that this fight would come down to the individual shark and bear, and the success of the initial attack.

We'll call it a draw.

GREAT WHITE vs ORCA

Since the great white versus the Kodiak bear match up ended in a tie, it seemed only fair to give the shark another chance. So we'll make it great white vs. orca—a match that could also happen in real life.

As the largest member of the dolphin family, orcas are often considered intelligent and friendly. Their black-and-white coloring is distinctive, making it easy for scientists to tell one orca apart from another for study. They're so beloved it's sometimes easy to forget that another name for them is killer whales—one they earned for being fierce predators.

Orcas swim in pods of up to 40, communicating with each other and taking a cooperative hunting approach. Because of this hunting style, they are often referred to as the "wolves of the sea." Adult orcas are surprisingly large—they can grow to be between 23–32 feet, and can weigh up to 11 tons. They can also reach speeds of 30 miles an hour. To top it off, orcas wield a formidable set of three-inch interlocking teeth.

Though these teeth make great weapons, the orca's biggest advantage is its big brain. This brain is the second largest among ocean mammals. Orcas put these giant brains to good use when they hunt, adapting different strategies for different prey and situations. For example, if they're hunting a seal that happens to be out of reach on an ice floe, they will swim right at the ice in a tight formation, creating their own wave. They give the water a final push with their tails right as they dive under the ice. The wave

crashes over and pushes the seal directly into the waiting orcas.

If they're hunting a larger whale, they work as a pod to chase it down, nipping and bumping it until it's exhausted. Then they launch themselves up and block the whale's blowhole from reaching the surface, repeating this maneuver until the whale finally drowns.

Orcas are also the only whales that intentionally beach themselves. They throw their large bodies on shore with a burst of speed to snatch a young seal off the beach. Then they shuffle themselves back into the water with their catch, sometimes releasing the seal temporarily so the juvenile orcas can practice their hunting skills. These are just a few of the tactics that make orcas such efficient killers.

As a reminder: the great white shark is a gigantic, solitary hunter that ambushes from below with torpedo-like speed and 300 razor-sharp teeth. Sneaky, fast, and powerful, great whites are a perfect apex predator and have almost no natural enemies.

Almost.

WHO WOULD WIN IN A FIGHT?

Orcas can take down great white sharks. It's dangerous business, but they can do it. When hunting a great white shark, a pod of orcas swims close, careful to avoid the great white's jaws. They use their tails to push the shark toward the surface, creating a vortex. Once there, the orcas slam their tails down on the shark's head.

After a few rounds of this, they use their tails to flip the shark over. Like many sharks, great whites fall victim to "tonic immobility," meaning that when they are turned over they go into a stupor. Limp and temporarily paralyzed, the shark is no longer dangerous to the orca. The pod can now safely eat their great white snack. Victory, orcas.

HAMMERHEAD ★ VS ★ WOLVERINE

A wolverine is what might result if a skunk and a bear fell in love and had a baby. Even though they are the biggest of the weasel family, wolverines aren't huge, measuring an average of 26–34 inches from snout to rump, or 33–44 inches if you count their tails. They weigh anywhere from 24–40 pounds, about as much as a human toddler.

But they're way fiercer than toddlers, built to thrive in a harsh and cold environment. Their paws spread out to double their size as they walk, making a natural snowshoe. They have such a keen sense of smell they can detect prey hiding under 20 feet of snow, which they blaze through with the big claws on their big paws.

They rip prey out of their dens and snap through bone, flesh, even frozen meat. Bones, meat, fur, teeth—you name it, they will eat it. Because even though they are omnivores, they will do just about anything for meat. Their scientific name, *Gulo gulo*, comes from the Latin word meaning "glutton."

Wolverines hunt at night, and while they usually stick to a diet of small mammals rounded out with plants and berries, they will take on larger prey like caribou, reindeer, and sheep—especially if these animals are sick or injured.

If possible, wolverines will skip the hunt altogether and wait for another predator to take down large prey. Then the wolverine chases off the predator with fierce snarls, growls, and a flash of fangs. Afterward, the wolverine chows down on its stolen meal, even hiding what it can't finish in the snow for later in its own creepy version of frozen dinners.

Hammerheads are every bit as memorable as wolverines. Their oddly shaped heads, known as cephalofoils, give them their name—and also give them a distinct advantage in the hunt. Having widespread eyes increases their visual range. With a flick to either side, the hammerhead can enjoy almost panoramic vision. They can also see in the dark. Their cephalofoils also contain sensory organs that help them track down their next meals. And the cephalofoil acts as a rudder, which lets the shark turn quickly, giving hammerheads the best maneuverability of any shark.

Great hammerheads, which are the largest hammerheads that we know, can grow as long as 20 feet and can weigh about 1,000 pounds. They have jagged, needlelike teeth to tear into stingrays, which are their preferred diet. The hammerhead skims the sand, searching for the natural electric field the stingray gives off with its muscle contractions. Stingrays do have venomous spines for self-defense. But the hammerhead doesn't care: It's immune.

WHO WOULD WIN IN A FIGHT?

Tough call. Wolverines have poor eyesight, so it seems likely that the hammerhead would get first bite. If the hammerhead's attack mimicked that of its attack on a stingray, it would go for the wolverine's limbs first, quickly taking it down. With the hammerhead's superior eyesight and ability to sense electrical fields, it has a clear advantage over the wolverine. Even more important, the hammerhead has excellent night vision, which is when the wolverine prefers to hunt.

However, if the wolverine managed to avoid the initial rush, there's a possibility it would at least manage to limp away. Wolverines have powerful jaws and can eat bones, teeth, and meatsicles. If the wolverine managed to get hold of the shark's cephalofoil, it could easily crunch through it, digging in with its long claws as it did. The shark would most likely retreat and search for easier prey.

This fight is going down as a draw, though one in favor of the hammerhead.

SIBERIAN TIGER vs BULL SHARK

Tigers are the largest of the big cats, and the Siberian tiger is the largest of them all. Males average around 8–10 feet in length. They're three feet tall, and can weigh between 450–675 pounds, which is roughly the equivalent of two NFL linebackers and several buckets of chicken. Female Siberian tigers are smaller, about eight feet in length and 250–300 pounds.

They are solitary hunters, scent-marking large swaths of territory. They prefer to hunt at night, using their superior night vision and excellent sense of hearing. Well camouflaged, they stalk prey, and once their target is within range, they leap—up to 30 feet. Landing, they grab hold of their prey with their paws, which deliver a crushing blow, and then inflict grievous damage with their five-inch claws. Then they chomp down with their powerful canine teeth (averaging about three inches in length).

If their prey is small, they will snap the spinal cord right behind the skull. For larger creatures, the tigers clamp down on their throat, strangling their meal while also avoiding dangerous hooves and horns. Should they miss their prey on the initial leap, tigers can run up to 50 miles per hour for short distances, more than twice the speed of the world's fastest human.

Bull sharks are one of the most aggressive sharks in the ocean, mostly because of their indiscriminate eating habits. Bull sharks have a large and varied diet compared to most other sharks. This is partially because they live in a variety of conditions, often switching easily between freshwater and salt water, which is something most sharks can't do. This widens their hunting field. They will eat anything they can get their teeth on, even dolphins and other sharks. They're also one of the most likely shark species to bite humans.

Bull sharks are far from being the biggest shark. They have big, stocky bodies, usually in the 7–11.5 foot range, weighing up to around 500 pounds. Females are larger than males. Their dark dorsal sides help them blend in with the seafloor, making it easier for them to sneak up on their prey. Like many sharks, they're lighter on their bellies, obscuring them from below. Bull sharks have short, blunt snouts. They head-butt their prey before taking a bite.

WHO WOULD WIN IN A FIGHT?

These two are pretty evenly matched. If the shark was able to ambush the tiger while it was swimming, there's a good chance the bull shark would win. Bull sharks are tenacious and hang on to their prey.

However, tigers are fast, smart, powerful, and have long, sharp claws. The tiger could strike back and tear into the shark, flaying open its sides or damaging its sensitive gills or eyes. Tigers are also patient, willing to bite down and hold on for several minutes as their prey dies.

With all these factors in mind, we're going to call this one a tie, but with the edge to the tiger.

SHORTFIN MAKO ★ VS ★ CROCODILE

The saltwater crocodile is the largest of all crocs. They have been measured at up to 20 feet long and weighing 2,000 pounds. Crocodiles don't chew. Instead they snap up their prey, crush it in their mighty jaws, and then swallow the chunks.

Their jaws are powerful, indeed. Depending on their size, they can produce 2,500–5,000 pounds per square inch of force. To give you some idea how much that is, a human bite produces about 100 pounds per square inch. Remember that time someone bit you in kindergarten and how much that hurt? A crocodile bite would be that times 50, and they can easily take off your arm while they do it.

Surprisingly, crocodile jaws are much stronger closing than when opening, which is why you see wildlife officials taping or rubber banding a crocodile's mouth closed to make it relatively safe to handle.

Crocodiles have an excellent sense of hearing and they are strong swimmers. A crocodile can manage 20 miles per hour in the water, and 11 miles per hour on land.

Crocodiles are opportunistic hunters. They will patiently hide just beneath the water and wait for a snack to come by for a drink of water. Then they explode from the water with a push of their mighty tail and grab their meal. Once they have their prey in their jaws, they pull their victim back into the water until it drowns. They can hold their breath for up to an hour, which is a huge advantage.

Then they eat their prey whole. On the menu: fish, monkeys, water buffalo, monkeys, wild boar, and sharks. Annually, they kill more than 2,000 people, making them far more dangerous to us than sharks.

The name *mako* is derived from the Maori word for "shark," making this a "shark shark." The shortfin mako is the smaller of the two known species of mako shark, but is also far more abundant. The longfin mako, in contrast, is rarely seen. The males are much smaller than the females, averaging 10 feet in length and weighing in at 300 pounds. The females average around 12.5–13 feet and can weigh up to 1,400 pounds.

The mako has a streamlined, torpedo-like body and scales that move to help cut down on drag.

Makos also have symmetrical caudal fins, all things that help make the mako the fastest shark. When hunting, it can reach speeds of 60 miles per hour!

It's also a very striking-looking shark, with large eyes, and deep purple and indigo tops, silver sides, and white underbellies. They also have knifelike teeth. The ones on their lower jaws are visible even when their mouths are closed. Makos are no slouch in the bite department—one chomp can generate about 4,000 pounds of force!

WHO WOULD WIN IN A FIGHT?

This battle would be close. Both creatures are fast, strong, and big and have a healthy bite. Makos definitely have enough bite strength and the perfect dagger-like teeth to crunch right through a croc's skin. Out of the two, the shark is faster by a good margin. If the mako had any hint of the crocodile being there, it could easily get away or avoid the crocodile and get in a bite of its own.

However, there are a few things the saltwater croc has in its favor. First is the way the crocodile hunts. It lies in wait for long spans of time, unmoving, looking much like harmless driftwood. It is likely that the mako wouldn't even see the crocodile coming until it was too late. Second, the mako is one of the few sharks that have to keep moving to breathe. All the crocodile would have to do is get that one crushing bite in and dive, then wait for the shark to drown. This battle is going to the saltwater crocodile.

CHAIN CATSHARK VS DACHSHUND IN A SHARK SUIT

Most people don't look at sharks and think "adorable," but the chain catshark is something stunning to behold. A black, chainlike pattern adorns its skin, and its yellow or green eyes have a distinctly feline appearance. Chain catsharks prefer deeper waters, usually hanging out between depths of 246–1,800 feet.

Using their unique skin as camouflage, they stay motionless on the seafloor, or in rock crags, blending in for protection as they hunt and eat squid, bony fish, crustaceans, and segmented marine worms.

On average, they're 14–20 inches long, maxing out at 23 inches. Their teeth are narrow and triangular, with smooth sides. Also known as the chain dogfish, these sharks are often kept in aquariums.

The standard dachshund has a friendly-enough reputation, but they were actually bred to hunt badgers. That's what their name in German means: "badger hunter." They run from eight to nine inches in height, and can be anywhere from 11–32 pounds. Their low-slung bodies makes them ideal for maneuvering into burrows and flushing out badgers.

Because of their shape and size, they don't lose any jaw or body strength while doing this. They have a great sense of smell, and a sharp, loud bark, which also helps them in their task. They are great diggers, and enthusiastic hunters. To prepare our dachshund for the hunt, we've dressed it in a shark costume.

WHO WOULD WIN IN A FIGHT?

If it came down to a cute-off, it would be tough to call a winner. Catsharks have such a striking appearance, while dachshunds, especially wearing shark costumes, make you go, "Awwwww!"

But this isn't that kind of fight.

No, these two are serious and here to rumble. While the chain catshark isn't known for its aggression, it also isn't known for being docile. Its main defense, though, is to hide, either on the seafloor or inside a rocky crag, using its distinctive coloring to blend in. Neither would work against a trained dachshund, even one humiliated by a shark costume. With the dachshund's keen sense of smell and digging ability, the chain catshark wouldn't stand a chance.

GUMMY SHARK VS GUMMY SHARK

Gummy sharks are slender houndsharks found in temperate waters of southern Australia. They're not huge—four to five and a half feet, with the females outgrowing their male counterparts. They often hang out in single-sex schools, and tend to be more active at night than during the day. They are named for their teeth, which are flat and have been compared to pavement. They use these unusual teeth to pulverize crabs, shrimp, and shellfish.

Gummy sharks are candy, usually bright blue in color and roughly four inches long. They do not have teeth. Their mouths cannot open. If you put them in salt water, they will sink and swell up a bit (not as much as they do in plain water).

WHO WOULD WIN IN A FIGHT?

Real live gummy sharks have teeth perfectly adapted to crush candy gummy sharks, which would offer minimal resistance. Sharks replace their teeth quickly enough that gummy sharks couldn't even stick between them for long or cause cavities, which is their primary means of defense.

Pectoral fins down, this match goes to the live gummy shark.

THE TEN DEADLIEST SHARKS

This probably won't shock you: the shark with the worst record of attacks on humans is the great white. Since the International Shark Attack File began keeping track of such things centuries ago, they've tallied more than 279 attacks by great whites.

These sharks are big, usually between 15–20 feet long, which is the size of a small moving truck. They pack more than 300 saw-edged teeth. They weigh more than 5,000 pounds (about as much as two Honda Civics). And they have such honed senses they can sense blood in the water from three miles away. It doesn't take a lot of blood, either: a single drop in a 25-gallon bucket is all it takes.

Great whites aren't the biggest shark, but they are the world's largest predatory fish, and they're found around the world in cooler, coastal waters. Not only can they swim 15 miles per hour, they can launch their entire bodies into the air when they're hunting, a move called breaching.

Here's what's surprising, though.

As of 2014, 201 of 279 people attacked by great whites lived. No one wants to be bitten by a shark, but even if you do find yourself in the jaws of a great white, you can be reassured that you are statistically likely to survive. Hooray!

In general, any shark greater than six feet long is likely to do some damage if it bites you, and as you can see from the top 10 sharks on the list, most are larger than that range.

Here's more information about the rest of the world's 10 most dangerous sharks, listed in order of how often humans have been bitten:

TIGER SHARK:

This huge, striped shark lives in temperate and tropical seas around the world. Females can get to be as long as 18 feet, while males tend to top out at 11.5 feet in length. Experts believe they are nocturnal and move to shallow waters at night. They're usually solitary creatures, but might eat in groups. Their young are born live in giant litters that range in size from 10 to 82 pups.

Tiger sharks are famous for eating pretty much anything: shark pups, sea turtles, marine mammals, sea snakes, birds, dead animals, and garbage (including nails, tires, and license plates). Tiger sharks are listed as near threatened because they get caught in fishing nets or are hunted for their fins.

BULL SHARKS:
Named for their big, blunt noses, bull sharks are found in the shallow, warm waters of every ocean. They can also tolerate brackish and freshwater and sometimes swim up rivers and tributaries. Ranging in size from 7–11.5 feet, they're fast and aggressive and they head-butt their prey before attacking. They have gray tops and white bellies, and their fins have dark tips, especially during their younger years. They're not endangered, although fishermen often seek them.

UNKNOWN:
Sometimes it's not possible to identify the shark in some attacks. This leaves a whole category of "unknown."

SAND TIGER:
Also called the spotted raggedtooth or grey nurse shark, the sand tiger ranges from 6.5–10.5 feet in length. As you might guess from the name "raggedtooth," sand tigers look scary, and because they survive well in captivity, are an aquarium favorite. Their teeth are long and curvy, and they're brownish gray on top and white beneath (sometimes they have spots). You can find them in warm and temperate waters in all the world's oceans but the central and eastern Pacific. They are the only shark known to gulp air at the surface, which they use to help themselves hover motionlessly when

hunting. They swim slowly, sometimes in schools of 20–80 sharks. Mostly, they eat small fish at night, but sometimes they eat crustaceans and squid. They are protected as a vulnerable species because of their low reproduction rate (they're not a fishing target for the most part). These sharks have two pups every other year, one from each uterus. The pups are fierce; an unborn one once bit a scientist who was rummaging around its mother's uterus. The embryos eat unfertilized eggs and smaller embryos (eating unfertilized eggs is called oophagy).

BLACKTIP:

Named for the distinctive markings on their fins, these sharks range from just under four feet long to a little over six feet (though some females can grow to more than eight feet in length). These sharks live in tropical and subtropical areas, traveling close to the shore of these warm water environments. They also travel near river mouths and in shallow, muddy bays, lagoons, and salty swamps (they can't tolerate freshwater). One cool thing about these sharks is that they're able to leap out of the water and spin, which is part of their hunting strategy. They're basically throwing themselves at schools of fish swimming near the surface. Another fascinating blacktip fact: in 2008, scientists confirmed a female blacktip impregnated herself. DNA tests confirmed she'd fertilized her own egg—a process called parthenogenesis. No one knows how rare this is. Blacktips give birth to live pups, usually in litters of four to ten, and the babies avoid becoming the meals of other sharks by living together in nurseries. The species is near threatened, because they are fished for their meat and fins.

BRONZE WHALER:

Named for its bronzy-olive color, these sharks are also called the narrowtooth or copper shark, and they grow to about seven to eight feet in length. They live in the Indo-Pacific, Atlantic, and Mediterranean seas (where waters are warm). They mostly like deep waters, but migrate to get to the saline levels they prefer. Younger ones can be found in shallower waters.

They eat cephalopods (such as squids and octo-puses), bony fish, smaller sharks, and rays, and they travel in groups for hunting. They are listed as a near-threatened species because they're fished for their meat and because their reproduction rates are low. A fun fact: They bite each other when they mate, and give birth to live pups after a 12- to 18-month gestation period.

WOBBEGONG:

There are seven species of wobbegongs, which live in the west Pacific Ocean from Australia to Japan. These small sharks, which grow to around four feet, have a distinctive flat shape and patterns meant to camouflage them. The patterns look like anything from snowflakes to spots and even flowers. Their upper jaws have two rows of sharp teeth, while their lower jaws have three, and their big mouths have a sort of fringe around them made of lobes and nasal barbells. They crawl along the bottom of the ocean with their two front fins (and sometimes even crawl out of the water with these), eating crabs, lobsters, and octo-puses, as well as bottom-dwelling fish as they hunt at night. The females reproduce by keeping eggs safe in their bodies until they hatch, and then they give birth to live pups. They are a near-threatened species.

HAMMERHEAD:

This shark, which includes nine different species, gets its name from the totally strange shape of its head, which looks like a hammer with an eyeball on each end. It's evolved this fantastic feature so it can better hunt. The wide-set eyes? Better to see its favorite prey, the stingray. The broad snout? Better to accommodate an array of prey-sensing ampullae of Lorenzini. These let them detect the electrical fields generated by potential prey, which they hold down on the bottom of the sea with their wide heads. These sharks range in size from around 13–20 feet, and they live in temperate and tropical waters around the world, both near the shore and in deeper waters. Their backs range from an olive green to gray-brown, while their bellies are off-white. Some species are endangered, and some are vulnerable.

SPINNER:

These pointy-nosed sharks live in the warm and temperate waters of the tropical Atlantic, the Mediterranean, and the Indo-west Pacific Oceans. They range in size from around five and a half to six and a half feet, and are sometimes confused with blacktip sharks because their fins also are dark on the edges. They live in subtropical regions within 40 degrees of the equator, and they get their name from the way they leap out of the water and spin when hunting small fish and cephalopods. Attacks on humans are rare, and none have been fatal because the spinner shark's teeth are really meant for smaller prey than people.

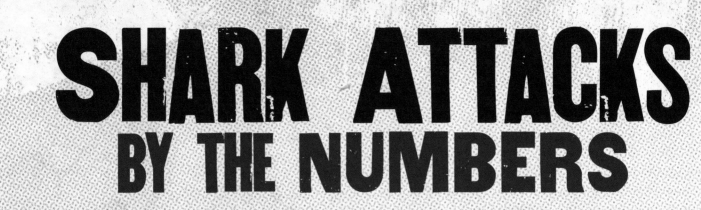

SHARK ATTACKS
BY THE NUMBERS

Once you read about a string of shark attacks in a particular state, it's easy to think that those are shark-infested waters to avoid forever. But this isn't how statistics work, and when you're making a decision about when and where to swim, statistics are your nerdy and helpful friend.

Using data from the Global Shark Attack File compiled by the Shark Research Institute in New Jersey, a state where you are more likely to die of an extreme reaction to an infection than from a shark bite, we've prepared an analysis of attacks around the world. Here are some highlights:

Of all the countries in the world, only 127 have recorded shark attacks (the records are inconsistent, but some go all the way back to the 1800s). There are only 12 countries that have more than 50 shark attacks on record:

UNITED STATES **NEW ZEALAND** **FIJI**

AUSTRALIA **BRAZIL** **THE PHILIPPINES**

SOUTH AFRICA **BAHAMAS** **RÉUNION**
(a French-occupied island in the Indian Ocean)

PAPUA, NEW GUINEA **MEXICO** **ITALY**

You have to take this with a tiny grain of salt because some disastrous attacks, like the sinking of the USS *Indianapolis* in 1945 (see page 105), aren't listed for some reason. Still, it's the best data we have.

Of these 12 countries, only two have recorded more than 1,000 shark attacks: the United States and Australia. (The United States is around 2,000, while Australia is around 1,240.) So by one measure—total attacks—the United States has the worst record out of any country in the world when it comes to this sort of thing.

There's another way to look at the data, though. The United States is also a very large country with many citizens. When you adjust for these factors, the United States ranks 44th in the world for shark attacks, just ahead of Croatia.

There's even another way to chew the stats. If you look at shark attacks that actually kill people, the United States is No. 51—so, just above average for shark attack deaths in countries that have experienced shark attacks.

So what are the worst countries per capita for

shark attacks? These tend to be small islands in warm climates—no shock, since sharks like warm waters. The worst in this regard are the Falkland Islands and British Indian Ocean Territory known as Chagos Islands, which are halfway between Kenya and Indonesia. Both are tiny, with fewer than 3,000 residents each. These two are so small that the single shark attack each tallied skewed the numbers.

So realistically, New Caledonia deserves the honors for shark-attack capital of the world. This country of 178,000 people is east of Australia and has recorded 46 shark attacks. Fifteen of those were fatal. To put it in perspective, you are 44 times more likely to be attacked by a shark in New Caledonia than you are in the United States.

The Bahamas are a runner-up. The Bahamian population of 359,000 has recorded 90 shark attacks. Nine of those were fatal. For perspective, this means you are 40 times more likely to be bitten by a shark in the Bahamas than you are in the United States.

It's worth pointing out that most shark attacks are not deadly. But for those that *do* kill people, the British Indian Ocean Territory once again tops the list. Its single shark attack was deadly, leading to a 100 percent mortality rate. An island called St. Helena, between Brazil and Angola, comes next.

But if we look at larger countries, those with more than a half million residents, and consider their rate of death by shark attack, a French-occupied island in the Indian Ocean named Réunion stands out. The island is populated by 845,000 people and has recorded 55 attacks. About half of those have been fatal. Perspective time: you are 64 times more likely to die of a shark attack in Réunion than you are in the United States. In fact, in 2015, swimming was banned there after what was described as an "invasion" of bull sharks, and after seven people died of shark bites over a period of four years.

Fiji also stands out. The population of this island east of Australia is 925,000. They've tallied 63 shark attacks. Of those, 22 were fatal.

COASTLINE DANGER

Another way of looking at the numbers is to consider how much coastline a country has, and not just its population. There's a reason there have been no shark attacks in Switzerland, Nepal, and Vatican City: all three are landlocked. Likewise, there are 90 countries with some stretch of coast that have recorded no attacks. Nothing magical is happening here—those countries happen to be too cold for sharks to thrive there.

So, while the United States has recorded the most shark attacks since 1900, the country actually ranks seventh when you take into account how much of the US is coastline—12,380 miles. It averages out to one shark attack for every 16 miles of coast.

Once again, that French territory of Réunion soars to the top. The attack-per-mile rate is nearly triple the attack rate in the United States (2.7 times, in fact). Réunion is also home to a higher proportion of fatal shark attacks—you're much more likely to die of one here than anywhere else in the world.

Again, the data are really skewed for countries with tiny bits of coastline that have seen shark attacks. Monaco, which has a mere two and a half miles of beach, has had a fatal attack and technically comes in second place by this measure. Right after that is Iraq, which has only 36 miles of coastline and a dozen recorded shark attacks.

Among countries with a lot of coastline (more than 1,000 miles of it), South Africa leads the shark attack race. The country has 1,738 miles of beach with 554 recorded attacks, which puts it at fourth overall in the world. It's also fourth overall for fatal shark attacks, with an average of one for every five miles of beach.

TOP 9 COUNTRIES FOR FATAL SHARK BITES*

*As measured per mile of beach

MONACO
RÉUNION
IRAQ
SOUTH AFRICA
GRENADA
SLOVENIA
SINGAPORE
BARBADOS
FIJI

TOP 9 COUNTRIES FOR SHARK ATTACKS*

*Per mile of beach

RÉUNION
MONACO
IRAQ
SOUTH AFRICA
BERMUDA
USA
FIJI
BARBADOS
AUSTRALIA

MOST SHARK-ATTACK-FREE BEACHES IN THE WORLD

There are 90 countries around the world that have beaches but no recorded shark attacks. If you don't mind cold water (sharks usually do), you can swim without worrying about shark attacks here:

DENMARK
ICELAND
ESTONIA

And you can swim in these beaches knowing that no one has died from a shark bite:

THE CAYMAN ISLANDS
THE VIRGIN ISLANDS
CURACAO
TRINIDAD & TOBAGO
THE COOK ISLANDS

The data above includes all shark bite incidents that have been reported. But to further put things in perspective, not all shark attacks are created equal. Researchers categorize them as provoked and unprovoked. An unprovoked attack is the sort you might worry about a tiny bit. These happen when you are minding your own business, swimming or surfing or what have you, and boom! You get bitten. Sometimes a shark doesn't even know it's biting a human (we're not a regular part of their diet). It just knows it's nudged something, possibly in sandy water with poor visibility, and it investigates with its mouth.

Other attacks are provoked. This isn't quite as bad as it sounds. Some attacks under the "provoked" umbrella are attacks on boats and corpses, and while both are unfortunate, we can probably agree they aren't as bad as bites to live swimmers.

Other provoked attacks happen when fishermen try to get sharks out of their nets. The last type of provoked attack legitimately raises eyebrows, and this is the sort that happens when people try to shoot or spear sharks, or when they try to film them or capture them for aquariums. It's not exactly an unexpected result. These are wild animals, after all.

So who provokes attacks? If you're looking at it by country, the United Kingdom leads the way. Her Majesty's citizens experienced 38 attacks, 16 of which were provoked. Two resulted in death. (The rate of death in James Bond movies, which are fictional, is higher, especially when laser beams are part of the equation.)

On the flip side, China leads the world for countries with unprovoked shark attacks. All but one of China's 28 recorded attacks were unprovoked, and 18 were deadly (a very high rate). China does lead the world in population and ranks 12th for the length of its coastline, so these numbers aren't quite as bad as they sound.

AN EXPLOSIVE SHARK ATTACK

The Lizard peninsula in Cornwall, England, has a nearby set of treacherous rocks called the Manacles. Not far from this site in the summer of 1956, two men died and another was injured in spectacular fashion after an encounter with a shark.

The day before the disaster, a shark had approached a nearby diver as if it were going to attack. The next day, another shark appeared so a diving officer named Lt. Commander Brooks, another sailor, and a pair of locals decided they'd scare the creature. They tied two blocks of explosives to a rope, lit them, and tossed them at the shark.

The rope caught the shark's dorsal fin or tail. Then the shark turned around and swam under the boat. The charges detonated and blew apart the boat. Two men died. So, presumably, did the shark.

SHARKS VERSUS TOURISTS

It's hard to think of a worse vacation souvenir than a shark bite. We wondered, when a shark attacks, how likely is it that the victim is a tourist? So we looked at the world's most popular destinations—those with more than 100,000 visits—and ranked them by shark attacks and fatalities. (It didn't feel fair to look at tiny countries visited by few tourists. A single shark attack there can really skew the data.)

For popular destinations, Australia—with more than 6 million visitors a year—is the No. 2 country in the world for shark attacks. South Africa, which attracts 9 million tourists a year, is comparable. The United States, which ranks second in visitors only to France at 67 million a year, is only 15th when it comes to the likelihood of a victim being a tourist. Apparently sharks prefer locally sourced humans.

WHAT IF YOU'RE TRAVELING OFF THE BEATEN PATH?

If your travels are taking you to Papua New Guinea, congratulations. This is No. 1 in the world for shark attacks per tourist and fatalities per tourist. (Over the years, there have been about 140 attacks with 55 fatalities in a country that attracts about 165,000 tourists annually.) New Caledonia, which sees 112,000 tourists per year, ranks second at 46 shark attacks, 15 of which were fatal.

For moderately popular destinations, Fiji and Brazil are tops. Fiji gets about 661,000 travelers annually. They've had 63 shark attacks, more than a third of which were fatal. Brazil sees about 567,000 tourist visits, with 99 shark attacks, only three of which were fatal.

COUNTRY	TOURIST ARRIVALS	TOTAL	PROVOKED	FATAL	ATTACKS PER 10,000 TOURISTS
PAPUA NEW GUINEA	165,000	140	12	55	8.4848
NEW CALEDONIA	112,000	46	0	15	4.1071
AUSTRALIA	6,146,000	1237	124	279	2.0127
VANUATU	108,000	14	1	9	1.2963
FRENCH POLYNESIA	169,000	18	2	2	1.0651
FIJI	661,000	63	2	22	0.9531
SAMOA	126,000	8	1	2	0.6349
BERMUDA	232,000	14	2	1	0.6034
SOUTH AFRICA	9,188,000	554	54	104	0.6030
NEW ZEALAND	2,473,000	124	19	26	0.5014
PALAU	119,000	5	1	0	4.202
SEYCHELLES	208,000	8	0	5	3.846
GRENADA	116,000	4	0	3	3.448
UNITED STATES	66,969,000	1999	198	161	2.985

HISTORY'S WORST SHARK ATTACK?

There's really no such thing as a good shark attack (for anyone but the shark that gets a life-sustaining meal out of it).

A shark attack doesn't have to kill a lot of people to be terrible. Though there's only ever been one fatal attack in the wealthy kingdom of Monaco, making its small beach the deadliest per mile in the world, a little boy was killed in it—making it a tragedy for everyone who knew him.

So how do you measure the worst shark attack ever—by the sadness of the loss? The gruesomeness of the bite? Or the total body count?

They're all terrible. But here are some of the worst to consider:

THE *LA SEYNE* STEAMER CRASH OF 1909

On a foggy Sunday morning in November 1909, a French steamer ship named *La Seyne* was on its way from Java to Singapore when it crashed with a British-India Steam Navigation Company liner named the *Onda*. They were 28 miles from land, and the French ship went down in mere minutes. The crew of the *Onda* pulled 61 passengers from the water, but they couldn't save everyone.

As an Australian newspaper reported, "A good many of the few who managed to scramble on deck must have been imprisoned under the ship's awnings, and it is also clear from what follows that of those who got clear of the ship a good many were the victims of the sharks in which those waters abound."

THE REAL NEW JERSEY JAWS

There was a heat wave during the summer of 1916 in New Jersey. A 10-day blitz of scorching temperatures drove many people to the shore—and five sharks attacked swimmers trying to cool off. A 25-year-old man named Charles Vansant was the first to die as he enjoyed an evening swim. Five days later, Charles Bruder died in an attack off the beach at Spring Lake. Three more attacks happened 30 miles north, at Matawan Creek. Only one of the five lived.

TRAGEDY FOR FAMILIES

Another pair of attacks, separated by years and miles, is heartbreaking because of circumstances.

In 1985, an Australian mom named Shirley Ann Durdin was snorkeling and scooping up scallops when a great white attacked her from out of nowhere as her poor family witnessed.

In 2011, Ian Redmond was on his honeymoon on Lazio beach in the Seychelles. He was snorkeling while his bride sunbathed. A shark bit off his arm and leg. He was rescued by a boater, but bled to death on the beach, despite the best efforts of a doctor who was there. It's hard to imagine a more heartbreaking end to a honeymoon.

THE SINKING OF THE USS *INDIANAPOLIS*

World War II was almost over on July 25, 1945. Germany had surrendered, and in just 38 days, Japan would do the same, following the nuclear attacks on Hiroshima and Nagasaki. The USS *Indianapolis* had played an important role in ending the war. The ship delivered key parts of the first working atomic bomb in the world to Tinian, an island in the Pacific. Then it was sent to Leyte Gulf in the Philippines to meet the USS *Idaho* in preparation for the invasion of Japan.

On July 30, though, just after midnight, a Japanese submarine torpedoed the ship—twice. It was a terrible attack. The first torpedo blasted almost 65 feet of the ship's bow out of the water. It set fire to a tank filled with thousands of gallons of aviation fuel. This blew a tower of flame high into the sky. The second torpedo struck near the middle of the boat. It hit more fuel tanks and storage for gunpowder, touching off explosions that ripped the boat in half.

Many of the nearly 1,200 sailors on board went down with the ship—an estimated 300. But more survived the initial impact, the explosions, and fires only to land in the waters of the Pacific, which were known by sailors to be teeming with sharks.

There weren't life rafts enough for everyone. The lucky few who had them scavenged life jackets off the bodies of the dead and distributed them to the 300-some men who had to bob in the open water while they waited for rescue, fighting the thirst, exposure, and hungry oceanic whitetip sharks that had been attracted by the explosions and the blood in the water—not to mention the movement of the men.

Oceanic whitetip sharks are aggressive hunters. The night of the disaster, they ate floating corpses. But at dawn, they turned their attention to the survivors using their finely honed hunting instincts. Bleeding sailors were especially vulnerable. Survivors pushed corpses toward the sharks, hoping to save themselves.

As they waited for days, the men were hungry, thirsty, and every moment in fear for their lives. Even survivors with food to eat were in danger. One group opened a can of processed lunchmeat called Spam and the sharks went wild for it. They sank their rations rather than risk this again.

It took four days for the navy to send rescuers. A lot of men died of heat and thirst. Some went mad and drank salt water, dragging their friends down with them. The navy had snagged a message from the Japanese describing the destruction of the ship, but officials worried it was a ruse meant to ambush rescuers.

The navy pilot who spotted the men from above disobeyed orders and landed in the shark-infested waters to save the men in the most danger. Later that night, the USS *Doyle* arrived to complete the rescue of the survivors. Only 317 of the 1,196 men originally on board survived. Sharks might have killed as many as 150 of the men—mere weeks before they could have gone home from the war once and for all.

MOST BITES: ACCIDENTAL

More people die annually from electrocution by Christmas tree lights than from shark attacks, according to the National Oceanic and Atmospheric Administration. You never read headlines about the attack of Christmas lights, though. You also never see dramatic news coverage of vicious cow attacks in meadows. And yet cows kill many more people a year than sharks do.

The Centers for Disease Control, which keep track of all sorts of statistics about death and sickness, studied how deadly cows were to humans in four states over a period of five years. In those four states—Iowa, Kansas, Missouri, and Nebraska—an average of around 20 people each year lost their lives to the hooves and horns of cows. The deaths were horrible. All but one involved trauma to the head or chest. And many of the animals, about a third, had been aggressive before turning deadly.

But have cows had anywhere near as bad of media coverage?

Not even close. If you have long eyelashes and lack fangs, you have a much better chance of being deemed sweet and lovable, apparently.

Humans are not a typical part of the shark diet. Sharks generally don't hunt people, and experts believe that in most attacks, sharks have mistaken people for other food sources. It's easy to see how this might happen. Some sharks do eat marine mammals, for example. A surfer in a wetsuit might resemble a seal. They also eat fish, and

brightly glinting jewelry could look like scales. Certain types of sharks such as flattened angelsharks and wobbegongs live on the bottom and are well camouflaged, and might bite when stepped on.

Often after a shark bites a human and determines it's not the usual food, it will let go. But when the biter is a bull, tiger, or great white shark, it will be big enough to cause serious if not fatal damage. These bites are rare, but they happen, which is why it's never a good idea to provoke a shark.

Some sharks might acquire a taste for human flesh, though. Certainly the oceanic whitetip sharks that hounded the poor sailors of the USS *Indianapolis* were not accidentally doing so for four days. What's more, researchers in Mexico are studying this very issue for the most gruesome of reasons. Two surfers died in an area where criminals have been dumping murder victims. José Leonardo Castillo-Geniz, who is the chief shark investigator for National Fisheries Institute Mexico, is trying to understand whether the sharks there are figuring out that humans are, indeed, fit for eating.

Who's more to blame here, though—sharks? Or the human criminals dumping their victims overboard?

HOW SHARKS BITE
THE REAL JAWS

Open your mouth. Go ahead. Notice that your lower jaw is the one that moves. This is because your upper jaw is part of your skull. Mammals and fish that get their internal structure from bones have this in common.

Sharks, which get their structure from cartilage, have a different sort of jaw. The upper one can move all by itself.

Why is this a big deal? It means the upper and lower jaws can turn away from the shark's skull while it eats—and this gives it a bigger bite (or, if the shark is a suction feeder, lets it hang on better). So it's not just shark teeth that give these animals such spectacular mouths. It's their jaw structure, which has evolved to make them magnificent biters.

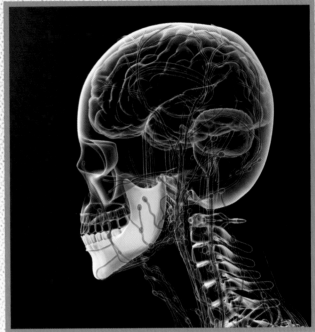

The many different kinds of sharks have something else in common. They all have rows and rows

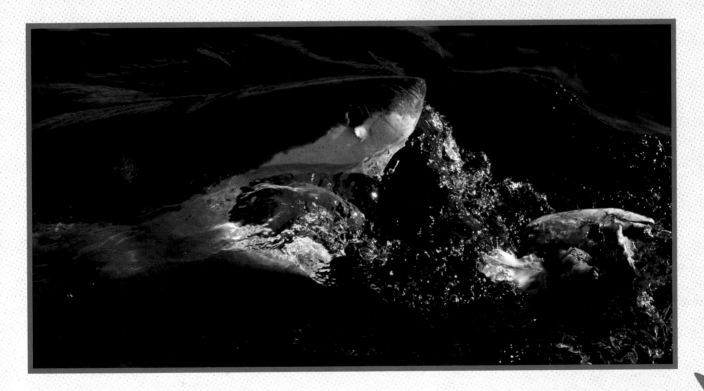

of teeth on both their top and bottom jaws. Like human teeth, which are the hardest substance in your body, shark teeth are really hard.

But you will only have 32 adult teeth in your life, if your teeth are typical (some people don't get all of their teeth, and some develop extras). In comparison, shark teeth are a wonder. They get new teeth all the time, and these form behind the old ones and slide forward, like replacement athletes coming off a bench.

Some teeth last only a few days. Some last a few months. But over the life span of a shark, which can easily top 40 years, that adds up to a ton of teeth.

AVOID THOSE JAWS!
HOW TO DODGE A SHARK ATTACK

Shark attacks on humans are extremely rare. On average, there are about 19 shark attacks a year. In contrast, ladders kill 300 Americans a year. Accidental poisonings are vastly more common. In 2013, 38,851 people died this way. That's even more than died in car accidents, and you probably never worry about your risk of dying from poison, and rarely think about dying in a car wreck.

If you want to worry about being injured near the water, worry about your toilet. That's right, your toilet. In 2008, almost 33,000 Americans were injured by toilets. In that same year, sharks injured 13 people.

More than 87,000 were hurt taking baths or showers, or climbing in and out of the tub. But does the thought of a toilet or bathtub make you break out into a cold sweat? We didn't think so (which is good, because you'd have to rinse that sweat off somehow).

You are almost certainly never going to come nose-to-snorkel with a shark in the wild, but just in case it does happen, here are some tips to keep in mind:

AVOID THEM ALTOGETHER!

The best way to avoid becoming a shark snack is to not to put yourself in the path of a hungry shark. We're not suggesting you never enter the water again, but there are some things you can do to make your swim safer.

CHOOSE YOUR SWIMMING SPOTS WITH CARE.

This is one reason swimming by river mouths can be so dangerous. The water there is murky, and sharks can't see you as well. Human activity—splashing around, bathing, and washing clothes—makes this worse. This can make a shark think you're wounded prey. What's more, you're also at more risk if you can't see the shark.

Most shark attacks are a case of mistaken identity. Unless you have the bad luck to run into a tiger shark or a great white—two of the more aggressive kinds of sharks—you're probably going to get away with an exploratory bite at worst. Sharks don't have hands to feel out an object, so they bump it in order to figure out if it's a possible meal or not. This happens when they are curious, usually while in a circling pattern and typically in deepwater scenarios.

Shark bumps can hurt you. Sharkskin is extremely abrasive. But their bites are definitely worse than their bumps. Most of a shark's brain is given over to detecting prey, and if a shark thinks you're it, you might suffer an exploratory bite. If it's a big shark, it could be a severe problem.

AVOID FISHERMEN AND FISHING BOATS.

It doesn't matter whether it's big commercial fishing boats, a few people on the riverbank casting their lines, or someone spearfishing. The fish will thrash around. While the fish are thrashing they are releasing fluids, acids, and blood—all things that ring a sensory dinner bell for sharks. And then there's the stuff that goes with fishing: the gutting and cleaning, the tossing of waste products back into the water. All of it attracts sharks.

So does blood, so avoid swimming if you're bleeding. If you have an open wound before you go in, if you're menstruating, or cut yourself while swimming, it's best to leave or avoid the water. But did you know that you're just as likely to draw the shark if you're peeing in the water? It's true. It's also gross.

PAY ATTENTION TO WHAT YOU'RE WEARING.

Bright or contrasting clothing and shiny jewelry can make you look like prey. Also, you look more vulnerable to a shark if you're alone, so swim in pairs or groups.

CHOOSE YOUR TIME WISELY. Avoid early morning

or dusk. (It goes without saying that you should avoid night swimming in general, but especially in waters that are shark habitats.) During the early morning and dusk the light quality is poor, and it goes back to that problem of poor visibility for the shark. If they can't see you clearly, they might take a bite just to see whether you're edible.

CHECK THE LOCAL NEWS BEFORE YOU GO SWIMMING.

If there has been a recent spate of shark attacks in the area, stay out of the water. Sharks will return to areas where they've found food before, just like any other predator. Don't think you're safe just because you're up river. Bull sharks, for example, can thrive in salt water and freshwater. They have been spotted in the Mississippi River as far up as Illinois! So it's worth doing a little research before you dip a toe in.

IF YOU COME FACE-TO-SNOUT WITH A SHARK

Even if you do your homework and make good choices, you still might find yourself uncomfortably close to a hungry shark. You are, after all, intruding on their habitat, and sharks are wild creatures.

So what do you do?

DON'T PANIC. Remember what we said earlier about splashing around? You don't want to mimic prey behavior. If you're splashing around like a wounded seal, you're interesting to the shark. Sharks don't have hands or paws, so that just leaves one way for it to investigate the situation . . . with its mouth.

Unless it's an aggressive breed or a tiger or bull shark, which will eat just about anything, the shark will swim off if it determines you're not a meal. A test bite from a shark can still be deadly, though, so it's best to avoid those teeth altogether.

DON'T LOOK AWAY. Sharks tend to be ambush predators. They want to sneak up on their meals and take them unaware. If you maintain eye contact, a shark will be less comfortable attacking you. Turn your head or angle your body to keep the shark in your line of sight. If you're underwater and there's a reef or rock face handy, slowly back up against it. That will make it easier to keep the shark in sight, and it will protect you from an attack from behind.

GO BIG. You can't convince the shark that you're not food. You can sometimes tell a shark is going to

attack. It might hunch its back, lower its pectoral fins, or swim in a zigzag. If a shark is determined to attack, you're going to have to go on the offensive. You will look more formidable if you stretch out and make yourself as big as possible.

GO SMALL.
If the shark is passing through instead of coming right at you, then minimize your presence. Curl up. This way, you won't look like food or competition for food. But don't play dead. This works with some predators, but not with sharks. In fact, if you play dead, the shark will think it's chow time. They eat dead animals regularly.

If you can, swim away. While you'll be tempted to sprint off, don't. Lots of movement and noise will only draw the shark to you. Keeping the shark in your sight, gradually swim backward toward shore. That way you're maintaining eye contact (or at the very least you know where the shark is) while you

swim. Keep this up until you are out of the water. Even large sharks can bite in fairly shallow depths.

IN CASE THE WORST HAPPENS.
If a shark does attack, fight back. Aim for sensitive spots, including the nose. But don't try to land a punch. Next time you're in a swimming pool, go underwater and try to throw one. You'll notice how hard it is. The water absorbs all the force behind your fist. A karate chop motion works better because your hand can slice through the water faster than your fist.

But be careful. Right under that sensitive shark snout is a mouth full of jagged teeth. When you're in the thick of battle with a shark, you might miss the nose altogether—which is a good way to lose an arm. You're better off aiming for the gills and eyes.

If you happen to have something with you—a camera, a snorkel, a mask, whatever—use that as

a defensive tool. It's safer to bop a shark with a camera, and it saves your skin from coming into contact with the shark's rough dermal denticles. Usually, pushing a shark away with an object is enough.

If a shark does bite you, grab on to it. Sharks whip their victims around to tear off chunks of meat, and you will be more likely to keep your limb if the shark can't do this.

Always, though, avoiding contact with sharks is better. Sharks are magnificent predators. Even its skin is a weapon, and if one bites you, you will be injured. Fortunately, though, you will probably never have to deal with this situation.

Far more common are human bites—which come right after cat and dog bites in frequency. One 1977 study in New York indicated city residents had a one in 10,000 chance of being bitten by a fellow human. Your odds of being bitten by a shark are one in 11.5 million (and your odds of dying from it are even lower still). Sharks are safer than other people. They're safer than toilets. Yes, they are deadly predators—but your chance of ever being harmed by one is practically zero.

CHAPTER FIVE

EVEN SHARKS HAVE ENEMIES

THREATS TO SHARKS

Sharks have outlasted dinosaurs, giant mammals, and terror birds. Although many species of shark have gone extinct in mass-extinction events during the Cretaceous, Triassic-Jurassic, Permian-Triassic, Devonian, and Ordovician-Silurian periods, hundreds of species of shark still remain on earth—many similar to ones that existed hundreds of millions of years ago.

That is changing, though. And unlike mass extinctions from the past, which followed natural climate change, the looming trouble in the ocean is happening with astonishing speed. Now many types of sharks are endangered—and human beings are to blame.

Three big human activities are putting sharks at risk: commercial shark fishing; accidental shark capture by fishermen; and the destruction the environment through pollution, habitat degradation, and human-caused climate change.

It also doesn't help that sharks have been misrepresented in the media as scary killers.

HOW BAD IS THE PERIL SHARKS FACE?

The International Union for Conservation of Nature has been keeping track of species and population data for just over 50 years. In 2014, the IUCN reported that one-quarter of all species of sharks and rays is now threatened with extinction (and it's worse for rays than for sharks).

The risk to sharks, rays, and chimaeras is "alarmingly elevated," according to an IUCN report, based on collaborative work by 302 experts in 64 countries.

"In greatest peril are the largest species of rays and sharks, especially those living in shallow water that is accessible to fisheries."

Being endangered and being threatened mean different things. An endangered species is a plant or animal that could die out in most or all of its habitat. Threatened species are ones that will become endangered within the foreseeable future.

It's hard to know which sharks are the most vulnerable. Some sharks we know so little about, we have no way of knowing whether they're in trouble. And there are almost certainly shark species we've never encountered that will become extinct before we do.

The fact is, many sharks are vulnerable due to fishing, finning, and habitat degradation and destruction.

There won't be any quick solutions to these problems, and they are compounded by the fact that sharks reproduce slowly. (They're different from bony fishes, which lay lots of eggs and reproduce themselves more quickly, and can bounce back faster from assaults like overfishing.)

In 2014, the scalloped hammerhead shark became the first species to be protected by the US Endangered Species Act, one of the strongest wildlife conservation laws in the world. This hammerhead is found in coastal warm, temperate, and tropical seas around the world, though, and will need protection everywhere to survive. Fishermen target hammerheads because their fins are desirable. They're also sometimes caught by accident. Because they're a fragile species, even the ones returned to the water don't always make it.

GREAT WHITE SHARKS
WHALE SHARKS
BASKING SHARKS
GANGES SHARKS
BORNEO SHARKS
ANGULAR ANGELSHARKS
PONDICHERRY SHARKS
SPEARTOOTH SHARKS
GULPER SHARKS
WHITEFIN SHARKS
SMOOTHBACK ANGELSHARKS
SPINNER SHARKS
DUSKY SHARKS
GREY NURSE SHARKS
TOPE SHARKS
PORBEAGLE SHARKS

With other sharks, we don't have enough data on their numbers to know whether they're in trouble. This list includes thresher sharks, Java sharks, kitefin sharks, salmon sharks, broadnose sevengills, bigeye sand tigers, narrowmouth catsharks, Argentine angelsharks, and megamouths.

This is one reason research is important: so we can better understand these animals, the threats to them, and what we can do to support them and keep them a thriving part of the ecosystem.

INACCURATE MOVIE PORTRAYALS

One thing that doesn't help the cause of sharks is inaccurate characterizations in the media. Many more people die from car accidents than from shark bites, but you wouldn't know this from the sensational headlines every time there is an attack—which was most likely a case of a shark thinking a person is something else. In part, this kind of coverage happens *because* shark bites are so unusual.

But in part, it's because we've been conditioned to fear sharks by things we've seen in the movies. A good movie or show can make us really feel scared. We can laugh authentic laughter and cry real tears. That's how we know the made-up thing we're watching is good. Even though it's all an illusion, we've bought into it completely.

This is a problem when we continue to believe even after the show has ended.

Take *Jaws*, for example. During the 1970s, when it came out, Hollywood was in a bit of a slump. Ticket prices were low. The country was enmeshed in the Vietnam War until the middle of the decade, and people weren't seeing movies like they used to.

Then came two action-packed, innovative flicks—*Jaws* and *Star Wars*. It felt as though everyone had seen these movies, and everyone was talking about them. Their success revitalized the movie industry, but even more, gave audiences things to obsess over. This was good for Jedis, but bad for the real-life jaws.

The movie made it seem as though the sharks were thinking, plotting villains—instead of animals doing what animals do in their natural habitats. As a result, people started hunting sharks, which is actually less of a challenge with great whites than you might think. They'll swim right up to a baited hook and bite.

The fear of great whites and other sharks after the movie became so great that the man who wrote the initial book and the screenplay that followed, Peter Benchley, became a shark conservationist. Before he died, Benchley told a London newspaper, "Knowing what I know now, I could never write that book today. Sharks don't target human beings, and they certainly don't hold grudges."

Humans do hold grudges, though, and we've definitely targeted sharks in part because of movies.

HERE ARE SOME MORE MISCONCEPTIONS CREATED BY JAWS:

- When there are several shark attacks in a row in the same area, it's most likely not one rogue shark.

- Oceanic whitetip sharks, not great whites, attacked the survivors of the USS *Indianapolis*.

- Great whites don't chew their food. So, Captain Quint wouldn't have gone down quite the way he did.

- Great whites don't have lifeless, black "doll" eyes. They have blue irises.

- Great whites don't attack boats as prey. They will nudge them to investigate.

- People are too bony for great whites, which typically eat blubbery marine mammals.

That said, not everything in *Jaws* was wrong. Most shark bites *do* happen in shallow water. Great whites also launch themselves out of the surface to investigate and sometimes kill prey. It's a spectacular sight. And they do ambush prey, as the shark in the movie was portrayed as doing (though not with the slow deliberateness of the movie—that was all done to get your heart pounding).

SHARKS AND JAMES BOND

Ian Fleming wrote the James Bond books that later became the movie franchise. He spent a great deal of time on Jamaica, snorkeling amid barracuda and sharks. He'd sometimes even go shark hunting. So it's no surprise that Jamaica and sharks would sometimes appear dramatically in his stories—and sometimes in silly ways.

For example, in *License to Kill*, a drug kingpin feeds Bond's sidekick Felix Leiter to a shark. The sidekick lives, minus an arm and a leg. This could happen. Most people who are bitten survive, even grievous wounds like amputation if they are treated quickly enough.

In *Live and Let Die*, Bond fights the villain Mr. Big underwater and, as tiger sharks approach, jams a

shark-gun pellet into the bad guy's mouth. The villain inflates like a balloon, pops, and rains scraps down (which the tiger sharks would definitely eat). The exploding shark-gun pellet is entirely fictional. Worse, though, is the idea of keeping tiger sharks in captivity. They rarely survive it.

In *The Spy Who Loved Me*, the villain has an elevator equipped with a trapdoor that deposits victims into a shark tank, where the waiting animals make quick work of the victims. If the victim thrashed or urinated or were menstruating, or some combination of the three, this might happen. All three things will attract the notice of sharks. And sharks in the tank could potentially take an exploratory bite, which could be deadly. But there is no species of shark that regularly eats people. Again, though, sharks tend not to fare well in captivity—even in the lairs of villains.

At the end of the movie, we meet a human named Jaws (because he has metal teeth). He escapes a shark attack by biting it. Sharkskin, which is typically covered in dermal denticles, would make this unlikely without causing damage to Jaws's lips and face.

In *For Your Eyes Only*, the villain drags Bond and his girlfriend along a coral reef, making them bleed with the intention of attracting sharks. A coral reef could definitely cause these injuries, and sharks could notice the blood and any thrashing. Bond got away in the movie, which is a realistic prospect.

SHARKNADO

The premise: a hurricane hits Los Angeles, causing tornadoes that suck sharks out of the ocean and deposit them on terrified victims on land.

This wouldn't happen, for many reasons, not the least of which is that a hurricane has never struck Los Angeles (they have arrived on land nearby, downgraded to tropical storms).

Tornadoes are powerful enough to pick up cows and other large animals. But great whites can't last long outside of the water. There's more oxygen in air than there is in water, they lack bones to support their body weight, and they overheat easily.

There *are* incidents where fish have rained from the sky, sometimes alive, though. In October 1951, this happened when a storm sucked fish from a lake in Macedonia, and again in 2010 in a remote north-central Australian town.

But most of *Sharknado* is exaggerated beyond belief. At best, it's in the so-bad-it's-good category. In one scene, a man is swallowed by a shark and cuts his way out with a chain saw (and retrieves another victim, still alive, in the process). This is beyond far-fetched.

And yet, there is a 2007 story of an Australian diver whose head, torso, and one arm were inside a great white. He fought the animal off with his free arm and an abalone chisel, and believes (probably correctly) that the shark mistook him for a seal.

FINDING NEMO

This Pixar classic has a subplot featuring three sharks—a mako, a great white, and a hammerhead—that strive to better themselves by becoming vegetarians. No sharks are vegetarians, though some eat plankton. Sharks are predators fulfilling a specific role in the food chain. It would be bad for the environment for them not to play their roles. Fish are food, not friends—at least for sharks.

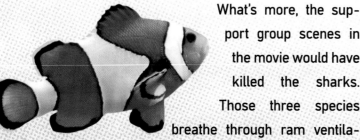

What's more, the support group scenes in the movie would have killed the sharks. Those three species breathe through ram ventilation, meaning they need to keep moving to pass water and the oxygen in it over their gills. They couldn't just hover the way they did. Nor would Bruce, the great white, have cared that he never knew his father. Sharks don't rear their young, and they often give birth in pupping grounds where males don't go so that the babies aren't eaten by older sharks.

It can be great fun to see sharks in movies. It's not something we get to see every day. Rather than getting overly scared, though, or losing our wonder at these magnificent predators, it's better to think about science and what's realistic. And if a movie makes you wonder something about the natural world, that's even better—you can use it as your inspiration to learn something new.

SHARKS IN STORIES

As often as sharks are portrayed in terrifying ways in movies, other stories show these animals in a different light.

In Fiji, fishermen revered a shark god named Dakuwaqa, a shape-shifting protector god whose true form was that of a muscle-bound man with the torso of a shark.

In Borneo, if you want to stop a baby from crying or keep a ghost out of a house, then you need the rostrum of a sawfish. These were traditionally nailed over doorways to repel ghosts, and wrapped in cloth and suspended over cribs to keep babies from crying.

Native Hawaiians called tiger sharks and great white sharks *niuhi*, and would sometimes eat shark eyeballs in the hopes of being able to see the future, or in the case of a pregnant queen, bearing a son with leadership qualities. The king born to that queen, King Kamehameha, was Hawaii's most famous.

One Hawaiian belief identified an *aumakua*—a benevolent guardian spirit—and sometimes this was the spirit of a dead ancestor reincarnated into a shark. There was mutual care between the *aumakua* and the humans. An aumakua shark might keep you safe in the water (and drive off bad sharks). Meanwhile, the family had to scrape barnacles off the protector shark's back and keep it safe and fed.

It shows a different relationship with the

predators than the typical one that appears in popular culture—one that acknowledges the danger that sharks can pose, but also the role they have in keeping the ecosystem balanced (and metaphorically if not literally protecting life with their presence).

It sounds like a small thing—the effect of stories. But if they help people respect and care for the environment and the complex web of plants and animals in it, then they are of great service. And almost no animals need this more than sharks.

WE'RE FISHING SHARKS TO DEATH

We are fishing sharks to death. In much of the world, there are no regulations about catching sharks. In the United States, some sharks can be legally caught. Some can't. And there are ways fishermen are supposed to process the sharks they catch.

Not everyone follows the rules, though, and each year, fishermen kill 100 million sharks (including sharks accidentally snared).

A 2013 study published in a journal called *Marine Policy* said this overfishing of sharks is pushing them closer to extinction. Researchers in the United States and Canada studied more than 100 papers to determine that too many sharks are being removed from the sea—30–60 percent more than can be replaced by their slow reproduction process.

This is just like spending more money faster than you earn it. Even if you start off with something in the bank, it will eventually run out.

Many of these sharks are slaughtered for their fins alone. Fins contain long fibers of collagen known

as ceratotrichia. These don't have any flavor, but they provide the texture of shark fin soup, which is one of the most expensive seafood dishes in the world. Shark fins used to be almost impossible to get, and the soup made from them was considered so special that it was served only at the banquets of Chinese emperors.

It's still the most valuable part of the shark—so valuable that sometimes the fins are sliced off sharks with hot blades. Then the sharks are dumped back into the ocean where they drown or bleed to death.

Many other products are made from shark, though, ranging from energy drinks to cosmetics and sunscreen, pet food, jewelry, leather, and food—sometimes disguised so consumers don't realize.

SPORT FISHING

Some people hunt sharks as trophies. Iconic species such as the great white are particularly vulnerable. Their numbers have dropped by more than 75 percent in the last 20 years along the Atlantic coast. Partly it's because they're getting snared in commercial fishing operations, but partly because of people selling fins and great white jaws. People are willing to pay as much as $500 for a tooth, or $25,000 for a great white jaw. The fin can sell for more than $300 a pound.

WHAT CAN WE DO?

It's not good for sharks or for fishermen to have the shark population killed faster than it can replace itself, which is why it's important to study the animals more closely to understand how and where they breed, and to protect them in all parts of their habitat. This will require international cooperation.

Mass extinction is a real threat facing many species. You can learn more about it from a Discovery film called *Racing Extinction*, a documentary by the Oscar-winning Louie Psihoyos, which pairs artists and activists with state-of-the-art equipment to show people what is happening to many species, and what we can do to change things. (Learn more and get involved at racingextinction.com.)

SOME SHARK FISHING IS CRIMINAL

There is a big market for shark fins in Asia, and people are willing to spend up to $100 on a bowl of soup thickened with strands of collagen from shark fins. Some estimates are as high as 100 million sharks a year being lost to the practice.

Stopping this gruesome trade requires more than just knowing how many sharks are dying. It's also understanding the market. As Asia's economy booms, more people are able to afford the expense of shark fin soup. Knowing who's buying and selling the fins is a crucial step to ending the practice.

A conservation group called Oceana found that

87 countries provide shark fins to Hong Kong, for example. The top provider, according to their report, was Spain, with 5.7 million pounds of shark fins in 2008. The US ranked seventh that year. This is information that can be used to persuade lawmakers to enact tougher regulations and punishments.

Political action is also important. Shark finning has been banned in 14 countries so far. Shark finning is regulated in 22 countries, including the United States. The sale of shark fins and other products that come from sharks is banned in 12 countries and states, including Washington, Oregon, California, Illinois, and Hawaii.

Although the regulations vary, they're generally meant to stop fishermen from slicing the fins off sharks and dropping their mortally wounded bodies back into the ocean. It doesn't mean shark fins still can't be acquired. In the United States, sharks must be landed on fishing boats with their fins fully or partially attached (except for smooth dogfish).

Unfortunately, though, not everyone is following laws regarding sharks and hunting them. In China, for example, it is illegal to hunt whale sharks, which is a protected species both in China and internationally. And yet, a three-year investigation discovered that a factory in southeastern China was butchering up to 600 of the animals a year. It's not hard to guess why people are willing to break the law. Each of those enormous sharks is worth about $30,000. Restaurants buy the fins for soup, consumers eat the meat, and manufacturers make bags out of the leather, and turn the oil into health supplements. The undercover investigation also found the same factory was processing great whites and basking sharks, which are also protected species.

Shark finning even has connections to organized crime. The celebrity chef Gordon Ramsay, known for his TV shows *Hell's Kitchen* and *Kitchen Nightmares*, made a documentary film about the international mafia that has grown up around it. Gangs from Taiwan and Indonesia are known to travel to Costa Rica, where they snag the fins from barbed-wire-surrounded forts and private docks.

Ramsay said some of the shark-fin mafia poured gasoline on him to stop his documentary and, another time, pointed guns at his film crew. He was eventually ordered to leave Costa Rica.

Interestingly, shark finning is banned there, along with importing and exporting fins. But this is what sometimes happens when lots of money is involved—people do what they can get away with.

ANOTHER WAY TO PROFIT FROM SHARKS

There are other ways of making a living from sharks that don't kill the animals—or necessarily even harm them. Shark tourism can be one of the most sustainable ways of using sharks to earn a living. Some studies have shown that fishing communities can even make more money helping people swim with sharks than they can by serving them up as soup.

There are dozens of countries that offer shark swimming and diving adventures, including ones that let you see blue sharks and makos on the East Coast, tiger sharks in the Bahamas, hammerheads in the Galapagos, and whale sharks in Mexico. The goal is to educate people and build an appreciation for these animals.

These dives can generate millions of dollars for the communities around the world. One study in 2011, for example, examined shark tourism in the Republic of Palau. This island country made $18 million in a year from shark diving, about $1.2 million of which paid salaries of local residents. This is far more than the $10,800 residents could have made selling shark fins.

There are some risks, though.

"Baiting" sharks is a necessity for shark diving. It's the only way tourists can be sure to actually see a shark. There are some potential benefits to the practice. Shark populations are down, and feeding them might bring them back to areas for breeding. But some worry this practice will train sharks to see people as a source of food, making them more likely to bite. It might also interfere with the sharks' hunting ability, making them dependent on handouts. Also, sharks seeking handouts can't tell one boat from another. The ones that get comfortable around humans can end up swimming right up to a finning boat, making their job all that much easier.

What's more, shark diving doesn't support all shark species equally. One study showed that bigger sharks tend to get all the bait, while smaller species suffer or even starve. In nature, it's generally better for animals to have to compete fairly for their food, as that's how specialized species survive. But if only certain species are advantaged, then the others fade away. This is called competitive exclusion. In the case of shark diving, this competitive exclusion is happening artificially because all the food is going to the big sharks.

Also, the "education" can perpetuate myths if not handled with care. Some tourism operations can sensationalize the dangers of swimming with sharks. Instead of going home and sharing how harmless sharks can be, tourists might instead spread the word of how they risked their lives by daring to dive with these killing machines.

Those concerns aside, it's far better to build an appreciation for sharks and an economy around them that does not depend on killing them. And you can manage the other concerns by choosing a responsible company if you ever choose to go diving with sharks.

THE PLANET IS IN PERIL

Even if all irresponsible fishing came to an end, other risks to sharks would remain. Our planet is getting warmer. This is called climate change. While the earth does change temperature naturally over long periods of time, the climate change we are experiencing today is rapid. Scientists almost universally agree that human activity is the cause.

Over the past 100 years or so, human beings have released lots of carbon dioxide and other greenhouse gases into the atmosphere. There are several ways we have done this: by burning fossil fuels; by chopping down forests that absorb carbon dioxide; and by rearing livestock that emit methane—in other words, cows that fart.

These gases wrap around the earth like a blanket, holding in heat. It's a big deal for all life on earth. Ice trapped at the poles is melting and will continue to do so. This will warm the ocean and make the water level rise. It could potentially flood coastal areas—including large cities.

Also, the ocean's chemistry is changing, becoming more acidic, which is not good for animals evolved for other conditions. We have already experienced more floods and droughts, as well as more intense rain and heat waves.

People who are not experts in such things have denied the truth of this for various reasons. Undoubtedly one reason is that it's scary to think about what it means for life on Earth.

Another reason is that people are confused by some of the terminology. *Global warming* describes how average temperatures on Earth have risen. *Climate change* describes long-term changes in temperature, precipitation, and wind patterns. Sometimes people hear about global warming but think major snowstorms are proof that it isn't happening. One United States senator even brought a snowball to the floor of the senate to prove it was a hoax. This is a misunderstanding of climate science. A warmer earth *can* make snowstorms worse, because warmer air can hold more moisture, and when it's cold enough to snow, more snow will fall.

Global warming and the related climate change are facts. There is overwhelming scientific evidence for this, and the wise thing to do is address it quickly and comprehensively.

WHAT GLOBAL WARMING MIGHT MEAN FOR SHARKS

One in four species of shark is at risk of extinction already. It's sad to think about animals never being seen again. But it goes beyond that sadness. Extinction of any animal in the food chain affects other animals in the food chain.

Let's say a shark that eats tuna dies out—whether it's been overfished or whether it's because the ocean has become too acidic for it to survive. Without this shark, there will be more tuna in the ocean. Those tuna not eaten by sharks eat more small fish, depleting their populations. Those small fish aren't there to eat algae, which smothers coral. The effects go on and on.

THE OCEANS ARE BECOMING MORE ACIDIC

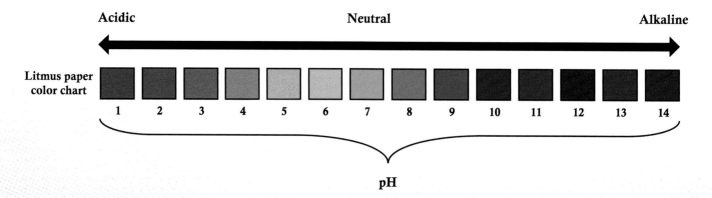

Acidic   Neutral   Alkaline

Litmus paper color chart

| 1 | 2 | 3 | 4 | 5 | 6 | 7 | 8 | 9 | 10 | 11 | 12 | 13 | 14 |

pH

Pure water has a pH of 7. This means it's neither an acid nor a base. Something that rates at 0 on the scale is the most acidic. Something that rates at 14 is the most basic.

The water in the ocean has a pH level of about 8.1. Before the Industrial Revolution, the ocean had a pH level of 8.2, according to the National Oceanic and Atmospheric Administration. By 2100, the ocean's pH level could be 7.7 or 7.8, experts predict.

This change has occurred because human activity has increased the amount of carbon dioxide in the atmosphere, which the ocean absorbs.

It sounds like a tiny difference, right? But it's not. The 0.1 drop we've already seen means the surface water in the ocean is 30 percent more acidic than before.

We don't yet know what effect this will have on sharks. The acid water is hard on some bony fish and not others. Perhaps the same will be true for sharks. It's something researchers are beginning to explore.

In one study at Sweden's University of Gothenburg, researchers conducted an experiment with 20 small-spotted catsharks, which are common and found throughout the Atlantic and Mediterranean. They put half in tanks with water that had an 8.1 pH, and half in tanks with water that was 7.7 pH. After four weeks, the sharks that had been exposed to more carbon dioxide had adjusted the levels of sodium and bicarbonate ions in their blood. This helped keep their blood chemistry stable.

But the sharks in the more acidic water behaved differently at night. They wouldn't stop swimming. The researchers observed that after weeks, the sharks did not manage to acclimate to the water, and the researchers thought the sharks might be looking for more suitable conditions.

Another study put epaulette sharks into water with less oxygen and more carbon dioxide. These sharks can already get by with less oxygen for short periods. That's good news for those species. But it doesn't necessarily mean the same is true for other sharks. Not does it mean that's true for the animals the epaulette shark eat. It means more study is required.

But one thing is certain in an age of climate change: increased acidity in seawater is more perilous for species that reproduce slowly, as sharks do, because it means there aren't as many generations born—generations that might adapt.

DOES CLIMATE CHANGE MEAN MORE SHARKS WILL BITE HUMANS?

The more humans and sharks interact, the more shark bites there will be. Some conditions related to climate change will put people and sharks in more frequent contact. For example, if it's been hot—as it was in 2015 in North and South Carolina—more people will want to cool off at the beach. Dry weather can also mean less freshwater has flowed into the ocean, making it warmer and saltier. Sharks like warm, salty water. They also like the bait that fishermen use. All of these things can line up to mean more bites.

SHARKS DO GET SICK

There's a myth that sharks don't get cancer—that they're perfect predators that nothing can kill. This isn't true. They do get cancer, despite their spectacular immune systems. And they suffer other assaults to their health, some natural, and some man-made.

A PLAGUE OF PINT-SIZE PARASITES

Parasites leech nutrients from one organism without doing anything in return for the host. They can't live independently from the host, and sometimes, they cause harm. Head lice is an example of a parasite that affects people. They won't kill you, but they're certainly unpleasant.

Sharks can get parasites, too. In fact, they're sometimes like parasite cruise ships, ferrying around all sorts of passengers as they cruise the sea. The parasites take many forms: crustaceans, worms, leeches, bivalves, and protozoans. They feed on everything from the sharks' lip mucus to the undigested food in their bellies.

People studying the parasites are looking at a variety of things to better understand sharks, their health, and the health of their environment:

- WHERE THE PARASITES LIVE

- HOW COMMON THE INFECTIONS ARE

- HOW THE TYPES OF PARASITES CHANGE BASED ON WHERE THE SHARKS LIVE

- WHETHER THE PARASITES AFFECT THE HOSTS' BEHAVIOR

- WHETHER THEY HARM THE SHARKS' IMMUNE SYSTEMS

- WHETHER SHARKS MIGRATE TO AREAS WITH FRESHWATER TO TRY TO SHED THE PARASITES

PARASITES, GROSS AND UP CLOSE

Some parasites live only on certain kinds of sharks. Bigeye sixgills, which have mesmerizing oval eyes, harbor flatworms called Monogeneans in their gill slits. These particular creatures don't live anywhere else in the world, or anywhere else on the shark. Parasites can specialize in other ways, too, by

attaching themselves to specific spots on their host shark: the gills, the fins, inside their mouths, gill arches, and noses, among other spots.

Even great whites get parasites, including ones that attach to their gills and hang off them like bits of yarn, parasites that gnaw away on the sharks' dorsal fins, ones that nestle between the sharks' teeth, and even some that rove their skin and feast on mucus.

The grossest parasite of all might be the *Ommatokoita elongata*, an inch-long copepod that permanently attaches itself to the eyeballs of the Greenland shark. In doing so, it destroys the sight of the shark, which relies on its other senses to navigate and hunt. The parasite dangles out of the eyeball sort of like an earring, and some have speculated that it actually lures fish toward the huge, slow-moving shark. That would make this a symbiotic relationship, which is one where both organisms benefit.

POLLUTION AND SHARKS

Humans have polluted the ocean so much that there are giant floating columns of trash in the Pacific, Atlantic, and Indian Oceans, as well as smaller ones along shipping routes in the North Sea.

These patches aren't like floating islands that you can see. They're more like a soup of pollution near the surface, made partly of confetti-like plastic bits, and part from chemical sludge and other debris gathered by the ocean currents. No one knows quite how large they are because the debris is often too small to be seen from boat decks, airplanes, or sat-ellites. The smallest estimates say the Pacific garbage patch, the largest of them, is the size of Texas.

A lot of this plastic breaks down into smaller and smaller pieces—some small enough to enter the food chain and harm animals. Some plastic does break down, leaving toxic chemicals behind.

Sharks are vulnerable to pollution, whether it comes from floating garbage, discarded fishing gear, pharmaceuticals leached into the water supply, or runoff from developed areas near shore. Sharks are at the top of the food chain, meaning the animals they consume have eaten smaller animals, and so on. The pollutants and toxins eaten by those smaller animals accumulate in the sharks' bodies and can harm their health. Extra chemicals in the water can also impede their ability to hunt.

The effects have been seen widely. For example,

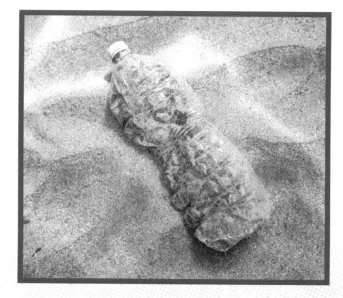

bull sharks in Florida have been shown to be contaminated with human medications that reach them through wastewater. And pollution and its effects travel far beyond local areas. Greenland sharks live in deep and remote northern waters, but even they are contaminated by human pollution.

SHARKS: UNEXPECTED ALLIES

Sharks play an extremely important role in the health of the oceans. But they can also help humans in many ways.

THEY CAN HELP US FIGHT DISEASE. We used to think sharks, because they are so ancient, have primitive immune systems. That isn't the case. They're highly evolved and specialized, and they can fight off harmful assaults quickly. Scientists have injected sharks with all sorts of nasty substances—things that cause cancer, virulent bacteria, and fungal toxins that would kill most other vertebrates. But the shark immune system prevailed.

The more we learn about how they work, the more new tools for fighting disease we'll have.

Tumors, particularly malignant ones, are rare in sharks (you can see samples of fish tumors, including shark tumors, in the Smithsonian). A tumor is a cluster of cells growing uncontrollably, and they are fed by nearby blood vessels. Tumors secrete a hormone called angiogenin. This makes blood vessels surround the tumor bringing nutrients and carrying away waste—essentially protecting it. Shark cartilage has a compound in it that inhibits this hormone. It starves the tumor and makes it choke on its own waste.

And that's not all. Researchers have found something called squalamine in the livers of dogfish. Squalamine fights off yellow fever, dengue fever, and all three kinds of hepatitis. These are all viruses, which sharks do not get, and difficult to treat in humans.

Shark blood also has compounds in it that prevent blood clots, and scientists are studying this to see if it can help people suffering from heart disease.

SHARKS CAN HELP US UNDERSTAND WHAT IS HAPPENING WITH OUR CLIMATE. From combating climate change to managing pollution, significant environmental challenges are ahead. We've long used animals to help gather data, and sharks are particularly useful for measuring weather and climate conditions. They dive deep and migrate over vast distances. Sharks that have been tagged can send data to satellites and back to researchers on land that tell us things we couldn't learn in any other way. They're the watchdogs of the sea.

Sharks also have fat that stores certain types of pollution, such as PCBs, in greater quantities than other animals do. A PCB is a human-made chemical. Until they were banned in 1979, they were used widely in pigments, dyes, carbonless copy paper, paints, electrical equipment, and more. PCBs cause cancer, reproductive problems, and other serious health woes. Even though they're banned, they can still sneak out of poorly maintained hazardous waste sites, and are sometimes dumped illegally. They don't break down easily and tend to linger, and when they're in the water, can spread over long distances. Sharks can help reveal the locations and extent of contaminations.

WHERE SHARKS ARE PROTECTED

For a long time, we didn't pay much attention to sharks. They weren't considered a useful resource. Many aren't good for eating because of the high concentration of urea in their flesh, a chemical compound found in urine that quickly breaks down into smelly and toxic ammonia.

As we have learned more about sharks, and about the importance of predators in ecosystem, we're no longer shrugging off these incredible creatures. Many conservation groups have formed, with people working in many ways to ensure the survival of as many sharks as possible—whether that's freeing sharks that are accidentally snared in the nets of fishermen, conducting field research, engaging in secret investigations, or lobbying governments around the world for better protections.

Saving them is challenging, though. Some threats, like global warming and the acidification of the ocean, are happening on a very large scale. Even smaller-scale efforts, such as habitat conservation, must be comprehensive. For example, if a shark migrates from one spot to another to reproduce, it doesn't solve the problem to protect them in only one area.

Knowledge is a huge part of the solution. The University of Florida's Museum of Natural History keeps track of shark attacks so we know how rare these really are (and how much more likely you are to be injured by a ladder). This helps eliminate unfounded fears that have been stoked by the entertainment industry.

Measuring the decline of sharks is also vital. It helps people understand the urgency of the problem. This is why in 2008 a researcher named Francesco Ferretti published a survey on sharks in the Mediterranean. Using log books from fishermen from all the way back to 1827, sales records, and other sources, they learned that sharks have nearly disappeared from the Mediterranean in just 150 to 200 years. The average numbers for each species here have declined by 97 percent. The numbers are alarming, and other researchers around the world

This fearful situation aside, there are good things happening for sharks and other sea life. Countries each have a 200-nautical-mile buffer from its coastline to the sea (or a neighboring country's coast, if they're landlocked). While most countries use these to generate income through fishing, drilling, and mining, some countries have set aside this entire area as sanctuaries. The 200 islands that make up Palau have done that, creating a 230,000-square-mile sanctuary. So have the Maldives, which means another 35,000-square-mile no-fishing zone.

There are also efforts to educate people who are eating shark fin soup about the problems associated with it. The retired Chinese professional basketball player Yao Ming starred in a very effective ad campaign about the damage the dish does.

And then there are things we can all do personally. We can take better care of the environment, burning less energy, consuming less, and recycling more. We can also do our best not to buy products made from sharks. If there is no market for them

HOW CAN YOU AVOID CONSUMING SHARK PRODUCTS?

Even if you don't eat shark fin soup, you might unknowingly be consuming shark. Many things are made from shark, including some seafood and sea-food substitutes that are probably unhealthy to eat anyway because of their high mercury content. Imitation crab and shrimp, rock salmon, and "white-fish" often contain shark.

In items like beauty products and health supple-ments, look for "squalene" as an ingredient. That comes from sharks. Some chondroitin supplements, meant to help joints, are made from shark cartilage. The idea behind these supplements is that sharks have terrific immune systems and healthy cartilage, and that we can boost our own health in a variety of ways by consuming products made of shark. This is a bit like thinking you can prevent aging by eating children. It's not scientific (and it didn't work out well for the witch in "Hansel and Gretel" anyway).

There is no doubt we can learn much about immunity and disease prevention from studying the immune systems of sharks—yet another reason to keep these wondrous animals alive, and thriving.

CHAPTER SIX

AMAZING SURVIVOR STORIES

EARLY SHARK ATTACK TALES

It's hard to say what the first shark attack in history is.

Many credit the Greek historian Herodotus with the first account. He was born around 2,500 years ago in Turkey, and wrote about sea creatures that laid waste to a fleet of Persian sailors. Their ships had crashed on the rocky shore of Athos, and had been broken to bits. Some sort of sea creature—they had no name for shark—"seized and devoured" the sailors.

It definitely sounds like a shark attack, and it's easy to see why there are so many sea monsters in Greek mythology.

BETHANY HAMILTON

One of Hawaii's top young surfers in 2003 was a 13-year-old girl named Bethany Hamilton. She went surfing on Kauai early in the morning on the last day of October. The water was clear, despite recent rainfall.

Even so, no one saw the tiger shark coming.

Hamilton's screams alerted people to the 7:30 a.m. attack. Eyewitnesses thought she was joking around until they saw her trying to paddle to shore with just one arm. Her left, she'd lost at the shoulder.

Other surfers helped her in, and the father of a friend she'd been surfing with used a surf leash as a tourniquet, saving her life.

The left side of her board bore witness to the attack: a 17-inch-wide bite.

But Hamilton survived—and then some. Within a month, she was surfing again. Within a year, she'd won her first national title. She later published a best-selling book about the experience and, in 2015, became a mother for the first time. These days, she's a professional surfer and motivational speaker.

MICK FANNING

Surfer Mick Fanning was in the final heat of a competition in South Africa in July 2015 when he tangled with a shark. Video cameras recorded the incident, and the coverage quickly went viral.

"I had this feeling that something was behind (me), and all of a sudden I felt like I started getting pulled underwater," he told journalists. "And then the thing came up and I was on my board and it was right there. I had this thought, 'What if it comes around for another go at me?' Before I knew it, the boat was there. . . . I can't believe it, I was tripping out. I'm totally tripping out."

He punched the shark and escaped with the severed leash of his surfboard. Safety boats pulled him from the water, and he and the other finalists decided to call the match a draw and split the prize money, rather than share the surf with a shark.

"I HAD THIS FEELING SOMETHING WAS BEHIND ME"

HENRI BOURCE

Henri Bource, a filmmaker, was diving near Lady Julia Percy Island off the coast of Victoria, Australia, on a November day in 1964. With friends, he'd planned to explore the island and film seals underwater.

Bource and some friends went for a dive around noon. As the cameras rolled, a large shark—possibly a white pointer—rose up from below and snatched Bource's lower left leg in its huge jaws.

Bource described the attack to a newspaper like this: "The shark started to drag me down. As I struggled to the surface I could feel my leg go."

The camera recorded the bite and the cloud of blood that followed. Companions pulled him from the water. They wrapped his bleeding leg in the rubber strip from a spear gun, keeping it tight using the handle of a knife.

He nearly died of blood loss. His doctor estimated he'd lost six and a half pints (the average adult has about ten pints of blood).

Undaunted, Bource returned to diving within a couple of months, called a "miracle man" by his doctors.

SIR BROOK WATSON

Long before there were such things as cameras, an American painter living in London unleashed a sensation in 1778 when he displayed a work called *Watson and the Shark*.

It depicted a 30-year-old shark attack on Brook Watson, an orphan and ship's crewmember, who'd been swimming in the harbor of Havana, Cuba, when a shark bit his right leg. In the struggle, Watson, just 14, went under. He surfaced briefly before the shark dragged him down again and severed his right foot.

A crewmate armed with a boat hook drove off the shark as it launched its third attack. The painting shows the shark, the boy, and the desperate rescuers, an extraordinary display of emotion for the time.

Watson lived to become a member of Parliament, as well as sheriff and ultimately Lord Mayor of London. Four years before he died in 1807, the one-time sailor and the first-known shark-bite survivor became a baronet.

PAUL DE GELDER

To be a diver for Australia's navy, you have to be extraordinarily fit and brave. Paul de Gelder, one such man, was at work in 2009 on a counterterrorism exercise in Sydney harbor when all his strength and courage was put to the test.

A bull shark attacked him from below, grabbing his right leg and hand with its powerful mouth.

"It shook me like a rag doll," he said. "I thought I was dead."

He had to get himself back to the boat, but he

couldn't feel his leg. "I took my arm out of the water and saw that my right hand was completely gone."

His medical training kicked in. He knew he had to keep his right hand elevated above his heart to minimize the bleeding as much as possible. He kept himself afloat and his arm raised, terrified the shark was going to return. The safety boat finally reached him, and his friends pulled him out.

The injuries very easily could have killed him. But his body was fit, and he could handle highly stressful events. His friends were also trained and knowledgeable about disasters, and one knew he'd have to pound de Gelder's heart to keep it beating.

Before the attack, de Gelder was terrified of sharks. Indeed, the attack was a nightmare come to life. But instead of becoming more scared, he has learned about sharks and their role in keeping the ocean healthy. He's even hosted a show about great whites during Shark Week.

And he's back in the navy, fitted with a prosthetic hand and leg, stronger and more knowledgeable than ever.

RODNEY FOX

In 1963, Australia's spearfishing champion, Rodney Fox, was defending the title he won the year before when he tangled with a great white shark. Fox, newly married to the love of his life, had everything to live for. He fought back after the shark clamped down on his torso, managing to spear the great white in the eye. It let go. Then it bit again, this time on Fox's arm. He pulled out. The shark attacked a third time, pulling him down to the ocean floor. Fox's body was torn open. His lung was pierced, his ribs were shattered, and he ruptured his spleen.

That he survived is remarkable. It took 462 stitches to piece his chest back together, and another 92 to repair his right arm and hand. The doctors couldn't fish one last shark tooth out of his wrist. There it remains. Not many people have survived worse shark-inflicted injuries.

Remarkably, this wasn't the end of Fox's

adventures underwater. A year later, he was taking top honors in spearfishing contests once again. He later drew up plans for a two-man cage that could be lowered underwater so people could observe sharks for the first time. After that, he helped Steven Spielberg film the underwater scenes of *Jaws* and,

with his son, has researched great whites and built a database of more than 1,000 individual sharks. What started as a terrible attack actually turned into something remarkable for both the man and the species involved.

AL BRENNEKA

It was 1976, a year after he'd been thrilled in the movie theater by *Jaws*, and Al Brenneka was surfing in Florida's Delray Beach, and enjoying a monster wave he'd just ridden to shore.

As he paddled back out for more, he felt something jerk his right arm—a lemon shark. He screamed and jammed his knee into the shark's gills, chasing it off, but no one came to his rescue. The other surfers on the beach, fearing Jaws, had fled in terror.

Brenneka made it to the beach and passed out from blood loss. The hospital pronounced him dead on arrival. But somehow, he squeaked through, comatose for three days. It had taken 20 pints of blood, twice what adults usually have in their entire bodies, to stop the blood flow. The bite cost him his

right arm at the elbow, and he needed skin grafts to cover the awful wound.

The experience terrified him, he told journalists. He knew what it felt to be stalked and hunted.

And at first, when he made his way back into the sea, he became a hunter of sharks, which he served to his friends. Then, a decade later, he caught a hammerhead, which was inedible and had to be dumped back into the water.

The moment changed him. He did not want to kill for no reason, especially an animal that hadn't threatened him in any way. He's worked as a shark conservationist ever since, tagging and releasing the ones he catches for the benefit of science.

CAMERON SUTHERLAND

Not every encounter with a shark ends in a horror. In 2015, a young fisherman in Sydney, Australia, was out in search of snapper in his boat when a large shadow rose up from the depths below his boat. Cameron Sutherland, 22, thought it was a whale.

It wasn't.

It was a shark, a huge one, longer than Sutherland's 18-foot fiberglass boat. The animal nudged the fragile boat's motor with its head, and Sutherland

knew its massive jaws could bite a hole in the hull at any moment.

As Sutherland often did when he fished, he had a video camera with him, so he lowered it into the water and captured footage that an expert identified later as a great white.

The experience filled him with wonder.

"He was so placid and gentle," Sutherland told the *Sydney Morning Herald.* "He was the king of the ocean; he could just destroy anything."

BITTEN BY THE SHARK BUG? EXPLORE MORE ONLINE!

SHARK BAY ECOSYSTEM RESEARCH PROJECT

www2.fiu.edu/~heithaus/SBERP/

Find research about tiger sharks and more wonderful sea creatures, with a focus on their habitat.

THE SHARK RESEARCH INSTITUTE

sharks.org

Find shark photos, videos, and more.

GLOBAL SHARK ATTACK FILE

sharkattackfile.net

Information about when and where shark bites to humans occur.

SHARK WEEK ON DISCOVERY KIDS

discoverykids.com/category/sharks/

Games, videos, apps, coloring pages, and lots of cool facts about sharks.

THE REEFQUEST CENTRE FOR SHARK RESEARCH

elasmo-research.org/index.html

Lots of information about the biology of sharks and rays, which are closely related.

THE SMITHSONIAN OCEAN PORTAL

ocean.si.edu/sharks

The answer to "What makes a shark a shark?" and more questions.

RACING EXTINCTION

racingextinction.com

A documentary that reveals two things that are killing off animal species—the international wildlife trade and the oil and gas industry.

DEFENDERS OF WILDLIFE SHARK PAGE

defenders.org/sharks/basic-facts

Facts about sharks along with ideas about how you can help protect them.

TOP 100 SHARK FACTS

discovery.com/tv-shows/shark-week/shark-facts/top-100-shark-facts/

Test your knowledge with this Discovery game.

PHOTO CREDITS

Together with our partners and viewers, we're setting out to make waves and build support for the conservation, preservation, and restoration of our planet's oceans.

To continue telling stories for generations to come, Discovery is making a commitment to supporting the conservation, preservation, and restoration of the planet's most precious resource, water. Change the Tide is an opportunity to make a positive impact on the waters that are so often the lead character in our stories. Simply put, a world without oceans is a world without Discovery.

CHANGETHETIDE.DISCOVERY.COM

INDEX